Steps for Life

A history of Cheshire Services Ethiopia
in celebration of its golden jubilee
1962-2012

by Robert Waterhouse

Published by Baquis Press

Acknowledgments and dedication

Attempting to cover five decades of a unique organisation in a short book is something of a challenge, given its unusual history and the scarcity of archive material. I've spent much of the past year in Ethiopia and the UK compiling this story. It could have happened only with the full cooperation of Cheshire Services Ethiopia (www.cheshireservicesethiopia.org), who took me wherever I wished to go and answered whatever I asked, and Leonard Cheshire Disability (www.lcdisability.org), whose librarian Jill Roberts opened the Derbyshire-based archive to me.

I have also to thank, in alphabetical order: Elfenesh Adane, Ian Breach, Sir David Goodall, Susan Hanf of Rotary International, Chris Love, Martha Mulageta and members of the Anglo-Ethiopian Society, Alan Ward

For the book's handsome design and production I'm indebted to Stealth, the Manchester design group, where Jill Taylor, Les Thompson, Pete Jolly and Jim Hollingshead allowed their collective arms to be twisted, with good grace.

Printing costs have been generously covered by Facing Africa (www.facingafrica.org), the UK-based organisation which leads corrective action in Ethiopia against devastating Noma facial disfigurement. Facing Africa's partnership with CSE is described on pages 82-85.

All opinions expressed in this book, apart from those attributed to others, are the author's. They do not necessarily reflect the views of CSE or LCD.

A few of the many volunteers, supporters and donors who helped Cheshire get established in Ethiopia and ensured its survival through thick and thin are mentioned in these pages. To countless others, Ethiopian and non-Ethiopian, who are not named here, this book is dedicated.

Robert Waterhouse, Manchester, July 2012

Published 2012 by Baquis Press Manchester M20 6AJ UK

Printed by Gutenberg Press, Malta
ISBN 978-0-9556025-1-1

Contents

4 **Foreword:** Myles A Wickstead
6 **Introduction:** the Group Captain's call from Addis Ababa
15 **Chapter one:** formative first years
22 **Aden to Eden:** the RAF fly in
24 **Produce or revenue:** Cheshire Home Farm
26 **Early fundraising:** income issues
32 **Profile Tsion Andom:** grand old lady
34 **Chapter two:** the Derg strikes
38 **Profile Mamo Eshete:** Mr Dependable
40 **Chapter three:** consequences of famine
45 **Chapter four:** into the modern world
46 **Profile Fr Colin Battell:** fighting his corner
48 **Rehabilitation:** core work of Menagesha
54 **Balcha:** the Russian connection
56 **Community-based rehab:** everyone's challenge
58 **Outpatient clinic:** adult issues
60 **Assessment and aftercare:** outreach lifeline
65 **Outreach in action:** report from 1995
67 **Beyond Addis Ababa:** Hawassa, gateway to the South
72 **Gebremedhin Bekele:** Leonard Cheshire's vision
75 **The annual walk:** changing times
78 **Profile Sir Alec Reed:** serial fundraiser
80 **Profile Lilla Heaslip:** creative networker
82 **Profile Facing Africa:** tackling noma
86 **Profile Nahu Senaye-Araya:** beyond polio
88 **Life story:** Elleni Moges
90 **Life story:** Sisay Nibretu
92 **Life story:** Aychech Molla
96 **Life story:** Berhanu Kifle
98 **Conclusion:** confronting disability
103 **Name index; picture credits**
104 **Children's thank you**

Pursuing Millennium goals

I met Leonard Cheshire only once, in the late 1980s. I remember little of what was discussed. But I recall very vividly his charm, his compassion and his commitment to making a difference.

The world has changed dramatically since that meeting. The Berlin Wall has fallen, the Cold War has come to an end. Some global risks remain high, and some, like terrorism, have increased greatly; but that of an all-out nuclear holocaust, which the Group Captain feared (with good reason) has diminished greatly.

This has created space to focus on other global challenges. The Millennium Development Goals (MDGs) were established in the wake of the Millennium Summit in 2000 with the objective of cutting dramatically the proportion of people living in absolute poverty; of reducing the number of mothers dying in childbirth; of getting more children to survive until their fifth birthdays and then getting them into school. And so on……

There has been remarkable progress against some of these MDGs in a number of countries, including Ethiopia. But as we approach the 2015 deadline for their achievement, significant challenges remain; in particular, ensuring that the very poorest, the most vulnerable and the most marginalised – including the disabled – are included.

When I travelled out to Ethiopia to take up my appointment as British Ambassador in November 2000, a significant proportion of the overnight flight comprised Alec Reed and supporters of his organisation, Ethiopiaid, out to visit Menagesha and other projects. I hosted a reception for them at the British Residence the following evening, all of us exhausted and exhilarated in equal measure. Ethiopiaid has been constant and consistent in its support. That was also the first occasion on which I met Lilla Heaslip and Gebremedhin Bekele, to whom Cheshire Services Ethiopia (CSE) owes so much.

I visited Menagesha on many occasions during my tenure, not least with HRH the Princess Royal when she came to Ethiopia in 2003.

I know that she admired what was being done there enormously, and that visit was certainly one of the highlights of CSE over the past 50 years.

This excellent history of CSE also gives us the opportunity to look forward over the next half century. CSE will certainly have a role to play in helping to secure a better quality of life for disabled people in Ethiopia, and I hope that the Government of Ethiopia will recognise the value of enhanced collaboration with CSE as the Ministry of Health rolls out its comprehensive and ambitious health strategy as part of its Growth and Transformation Plan. I hope too that the benefits of a burgeoning economy, with increasing numbers of wealthy individuals and companies in Ethiopia, are reflected in increased local support for CSE and less reliance on help from outside the country.

In any event, it is clear that CSE will continue to need – and, as is evident from these pages, thoroughly deserves – support for some time to come. We must continue to ensure that it gets it.

Myles A Wickstead CBE
HM Ambassador to Ethiopia, 2000-2004

"How utterly different, yet essentially the same, man is"

Leonard Cheshire's inherent humanity responded to calls from many parts of the globe. Among the first was Ethiopia

Early in 1961 Group Captain Leonard Cheshire VC received an unusual summons from Africa. Two members of the Ethiopian royal family, both grandchildren of Emperor Haile Selassie, invited him to visit Addis Ababa and discuss the establishment there of a Cheshire home for disabled children. The call came from Princess Seble Desta and her brother, Commander Iskinder Desta. This meant, of course, that their mother Princess Tenagnework was fully in the picture, and gave the initiative her full support. It would not have happened without the emperor's knowledge and backing.

Cheshire personally opened his first overseas homes in India during the 1950s. He already had an African foothold in Sierra Leone. Impulsive by nature, he was unlikely to turn down such an opportunity. He arrived in Addis in November 1961 on his way back from a visit to South Asia. By March 1962 the Cheshire Home for Retarded Children opened in part of a house in the Kisanchis district of Addis Ababa belonging to Princess Seble's sister, Princess Sophie, with three young patients, administered by a British nurse Cheshire had despatched, Denise Tabernacle. She had been given just £50 to get things going.

Leonard Cheshire was hardly methodical about the way he created Cheshire homes. As he recounts in *The Hidden World*, he was a patient at a sanatorium at Midhurst in Sussex recovering from TB in the left lung when, back in 1953, he received a letter from a Scotsman living in South India inquiring about the chances of Cheshire opening there. At the time the English operation based at Le Court in Hampshire was itself far from secure. But in December 1955 Cheshire left for India, completely unprepared – as he freely admitted – for the challenges ahead. His way of

Princess Tenagnework, Haile Selassie's eldest daughter, seen in a formal portrait, was the major benefactor of Cheshire Homes in Addis Ababa. She donated the estate which, as Menagesha, remains Cheshire's operational base. She also became patron of the Home. Her father, the emperor, himself a great supporter, invited children to his palace to celebrate his eightieth birthday in July 1972. Also in the picture are Gillian Hall, a volunteer physiotherapist (right) and Isaac Kifle, Cheshire's board member. In the bottom picture, Princess Tenagnework, along with her daughters (left to right) Princess Seble, Princess Sophie and Princess Ruth met with RAF volunteers from Aden when they flew in to help equip Menagesha in 1965

making something out of nothing by seizing opportunities and inspiring others somehow transposed to the sub-continent.

"For me," Cheshire wrote, "India was the school in which I learnt many lessons about how to work in another people's country. I first discovered how utterly different, and yet how essentially the same, man is the world over." Then he explained the modus operandi that applied to all his new homes, including Ethiopia. "If asked, we would send a trained nurse, experienced in working overseas, to move into the house which the local committee had acquired and take charge of the initial period of establishing it as a Home." After the first few years, Cheshire stipulated, it was up to those on the ground to take over. And so it proved with Ethiopia and Nurse Tabernacle, who in 1967 moved on and was not replaced.

Ethiopia in 1962 was a country of some 23 million people, ruled by Haile Selassie with what he believed was benign despotism. After acceding to the throne in 1930 he had set about modernising the trappings of an ancient kingdom, a process brought to a halt by Mussolini's 1935 invasion, the emperor's flight to Palestine, then to England, and Italian colonial rule. In fact the Italians, short as their occupation proved, brought new roads and gave Addis a bit of European glitter as well as their own version of repressive terror.

The Allies, moving on Ethiopia soon after Mussolini joined Hitler in 1940, swept to victory and reinstalled the emperor in 1941. Britain had led the operation and established what amounted to a colonial protectorate. Its influence irked Haile Selassie but diminished only slowly after the Second World War.

By the early 1960s the warning signs had been posted for Haile Selassie's regime. The ageing emperor still sought to carve a progressive image on the international stage, illustrated by the 1963 establishment of the Organisation of African Unity headquarters in Addis (the OAU's successor, the African Union, is today itself based in the Ethiopian capital).

CSE timeline

1961

Leonard Cheshire receives a call from Commander Iskinder (Alexander) Desta and Princess Seble Desta, grandchildren of Emperor Haile Selassie, to open a home for disabled children in Addis Ababa

Cheshire visits Addis in November 1961 and meets the royal family, who offer accommodation for the home

January 1962

Denise Tabernacle, a young British nurse, is sent by Cheshire to open the home. It is set up in Princess Sophie's Kasanchis house and takes in its first three children in March 1962

October 1962

The management committee of Cheshire Home for Retarded Children (as it was called) is established. The first chairman is Princess Seble

1963

Numbers grow so Princess Sophie offers her whole house, but the royal family requests a move. Princess Tenagnework, now patron of the Cheshire Homes Association, suggests an estate in her ownership at Gerfersa, later known as Menagesha

But in December 1960 senior officers of the emperor's bodyguard staged a coup which, although it failed, reflected serious misgivings about increasingly apparent social and economic disparities. Haile Selassie's British-educated grandchildren were examples of privileged status but at the same time naturally sympathetic to humanitarian initiatives. It's not surprising they were chosen to approach Leonard Cheshire.

Given the fate of the royal family under Colonel Mengistu Haile Mariam, a history of Cheshire in Ethiopia written in 1986 during the Derg years by an Addis Abba University student, Daniel Robel, offers a surprisingly generous interpretation of events. "Princess Seble and Commander Iskinder might have been genuinely aware of the needs of handicapped children, and concern for their needs could well have been the real motivation" Robel concluded.

No doubt an enormous care gap existed. Outside Addis Ababa medical facilities were sparse to say the least, while in Addis they were self-evidently inadequate for the growing urban communities. Cheshire's small venture in Ethiopia could hardly have been expected to impact on the problems.

All the same, it quickly incorporated the great and the good. The European community, alongside the Ethiopian élite and bodies like the Rotary Club, happily fund-raised under the first chairman, Princess Seble Desta herself. Organisational matters were sealed with the election of the first general committee in October 1962.

The Cheshire Home was, at first, a residential establishment for mentally-handicapped children, with Denise Tabernacle both the nurse and the matron. Numbers grew, and Princess Sophie surrendered the other half of her Kasanchis house, but soon wanted it back, and by the end of 1963 Princess Tenagnework was signalling that "their" home should move to an estate in her ownership some 30km outside Addis on the Ambo road. They called it Gerfersa. Others called it Kolobo. Today is known

November 1963
Visit by Margot Mason, Cheshire's general secretary, who reports: "Miss T is a good beggar and goes all out to get things for nothing"

1965
Wo Tsion Andom becomes chairman. Children now number 16. Flag Day raises $2,000. Contingent from RAF Khormaksar, Aden, fly in to help with building work, also donating £500 and a Land Rover. Two British volunteers create a farm, to which Princess Tenagnework gives five dairy cows.

December 1965
Haile Selassie and Leonard Cheshire officially inaugurate the new home at Menagesha

June 1966
Wo Makeda Aster Kiflegi becomes chairman

December 1966
Move to Menagesha completed. Children now number 24

January 1967
Denise Tabernacle leaves. She is not replaced by London but her role is taken by a volunteer, Mrs Stime, of the World Brotherhood Exchange

February/March 1968
Board of management created and draft constitution agreed

as Menagesha, the principal rehabilitation centre of Cheshire Services Ethiopia.

The story of Menagesha, and of Cheshire's extraordinary achievement in surviving (indeed, expanding within) the period from 1974 when the Derg took control of everything and Ethiopia was subjected to a period of genocide, will be told in subsequent chapters. It's a story with complications from a Cheshire standpoint because, in 1984, Leonard Cheshire returned with his wife Sue Ryder who had ambitions of her own for initiatives responding to the widespread famine. Various Cheshire establishments were grouped under a loose federation which eventually, in the 1990s, led to a split between what are now known as Cheshire Services Ethiopia (CSE) and Cheshire Foundation Ethiopia (CFE) whose activities are not explored in this book.

Gebremedhin Bekele, CSE's chief executive, is by far its longest-serving and most influential employee. He joined Cheshire as a young social worker back in 1973, just before the Derg took control of the country. After Europeans fled from revolutionary Ethiopia Gebremedhin, along with Mamo Eshete, the handyman at Menagesha, virtually kept the home going.

He also stood up to Leonard Cheshire in defending the Addis management board's decision that Menagesha become a rehabilitation centre for those recovering from polio operations (with stays limited to a few months) rather than a residential home. Cheshire had angrily declared that all his homes should offer people a haven for life. But he eventually agreed that Gebremedhin was right, and, true to his principle of self-determination, accepted the Ethiopian solution for Addis Ababa (most Cheshire homes around the world remain residential).

Self-determination has its consequences. A London-based global alliance of independent Cheshire homes is part of what's now known as

April 1968
New policy to admit only physically disabled children
July 1968
New policy to discharge rehabilitated children from Menagesha
1969
Cheshire day clinic opens at Asmara (Eritrea then a province of Ethiopia) offering rehabilitation after surgery at local hospitals attended by up to 75 children a day.
1971
Desta Girma becomes board chairman
Weekly polio clinic opens at the Ethio-Swedish Paediatric Clinic. Discharging policy allows 45 admissions. Expansion of Menagesha farm
1972
New dormitory building at Menagesha donated and opened by the emperor raises residential capacity to 80 children. Vocational training workshop produces orthopaedic fittings
Addis Ababa chosen by the Cheshire Foundation as headquarters of the Cheshire Homes Central African Region, with Fr Kevin Doheny its organising secretary.
Gebremedhin Bekele joins Cheshire as a young social worker

RAF work underway at Menagesha (see pages 22-23). From the early days, classroom education was always deemed important

1973
Isaac Kifle becomes board chairman
November 1973
Cheshire Central Regional Council conference held in Addis Ababa
Leonard Cheshire lays foundation stone of Asmara home
Cheshire Home opens at Gighessa, Shashamane, in cooperation with a Catholic mission. By 1976 there were 26 residential children with a variety of handicap

February 1974
Derg (committee) Communist revolution led by Mengistu Haile Mariam starts its activities
September 12 1974
Emperor Haile Selassie arrested. He dies in captivity the following year
November 1974
Commodore Iskinder Desta arrested, imprisoned in the Grand Palace, and is executed, along with 60 others, on November 23
Princess Tenagnework and her daughters Princess Seble and Princess Sophie will be arrested, then held in detention until 1989
1975
Expatriate volunteers start to leave Ethiopia
Wo Tsige Mengesha bequeaths a villa in Addis Ababa to Cheshire which later serves as admin HQ

Leonard Cheshire Disability (LCD), offering support and project-funding to its 53 affiliates worldwide. Cheshire Services Ethiopia (under its present and previous names) has received very little from London in pure cash terms. Gebremedhin's estimate of the sum is less than £20,000 over 50 years. LCD's regional headquarters, once intended for Addis, is nowadays in Nairobi.

Tanya Barron, international director of LCD, does not disagree that CSE is hardly near the top of her daily concerns. She stresses that CSE is fully independent, well-run and well-funded. She also notes that while LCD supports initiatives formulated around education and employment for the disabled, CSE's main drive over recent years has been rehabilitation.

Ethiopiaid, the London-based charity created by Sir Alec Reed and part of the Reed Foundation, has in effect been CSE's major donor for more than 15 years. Sir Alec acknowledges that CSE is among the best NGO operations in Ethiopia. As the founder of the Reed Executive Recruitment Group he likes to award points to his client organisations and CSE - along with the Fistula Hospital - is consistently among his highest scorers each year. Reed successfully raises funds for its Ethiopiaid operations by classic cold-canvassing techniques. However, he points out that there are worrying signs of donor fatigue when it comes to Ethiopia.

The issue is simple, the solutions less so. Since 1962, Ethiopia's population has soared from 21 million to nearly 94 million, with projections for 2022 – just ten years away – of between 110-115 million. In recent years, the Ethiopian economy has grown at around ten per cent annually, exceptional but in no way fast enough to catch up with the pressures of population growth. More mouths to feed, more children to educate, more old and sick people to care for. Ethiopia is no nearer to universal healthcare in 2012 than it was in 1962.

October 1975
First 21km fund-raising walk raises $8,000. Among the 199 participants who completed the route were six Cheshire children

March 1976
Cheshire Home for Physically Handicapped Children is registered with the revolutionary government to secure legal status

April 1976
Menagesha workers temporarily detain Cheshire chairman in protest at farm labourers' sacking and unsuccessfully call for nationalisation. Workers' unions control home for seven months

December 1977
Capt Alemayu Haile, Derg member and supporter of Cheshire, is accused of plotting against Mengistu and executed

1978
Assela Cheshire home for orphans and handicapped children opens, run by the Consolata Fathers

1980
Mekuria Tafessa becomes board chairman

1983-4
Ethiopian famine inspires Bob Geldof and others to Feed the World

February 1985
Ryder-Cheshire Ethiopia inaugurated during visit by Lady Sue Ryder and Ronald Travers, Cheshire Foundation international director. Its remit majors on a feeding programme. A centre is

All the same, CSE's contribution should not be belittled. Its strong presence in Ethiopia at the time when the global initiative to eradicate polio got underway in 1988 meant that most new polio cases have been diagnosed, properly treated and patients supported by community-based rehabilitation. Outreach teams visit remote rural areas regularly to check progress and make necessary adjustments to prosthetic equipment.

As a parallel initiative, CSE has opened branches in Hawassa, Harar and Dire Dawa – major urban centres in the south and east of the country. Workshop and physiotherapy facilities are supplemented by training and, most recently, seedcorn funding for income-generation; the aim is to draw the families of disabled people into commercial enterprises as a step towards "inclusiveness".

Fifty years ago Ethiopians typically believed that disability was a curse from God. Many of the first children at Menagesha had been dumped on the doorstep by those simply wishing to be rid of them. Management was soon forced to establish policies which ensured that children would return to parent or guardian after their operation and initial rehabilitation, a process normally taking six to nine months.

Under the system developed by Gebremedhin and colleagues, Menagesha accepts over 100 new cases a year. Now that the incidence of polio in Ethiopia is becoming rare, CSE is looking beyond clearing the backlog of operable patients. For example, it has entered a partnership with Facing Africa, the British-based NGO helping those with noma, a bacterial infection which ravages and disfigures people's faces. In February 2011 Facing Africa House was formally opened at Menagesha for pre-operative preparation and post-operative convalescence of noma patients.

Chris Lawrence, Facing Africa's founder, chairman and chief fundraiser, personally leads the missions in which teams of surgeons and medical/nursing staff fly twice a year to Addis Ababa to undertake reconstructive

---

planned at Mekanissa, Addis Ababa, which later becomes an extension of work at Menagesha

1985
Outreach services start from Menagesha

1986
Fr Colin Battell becomes board chairman

June 1986
Conference of Cheshire Homes in Ethiopia held attempting to coordinate initiatives

1988
Ethiopian Association of Cheshire Homes established
Global campaign to vaccinate against polio begins

1991
Fall of the Derg. Ethiopia will become a federal republic

1994
Yehualeshet Lemma becomes board chairman
Community-based rehabilitation project in poorest areas of Addis Ababa funded by Christoffel Blinden Mission

1996
Lilla Heaslip becomes board chairman

1997
Ethiopiaid becomes the principal sponsor of CSE after fact-finding visit by Alec Reed and colleagues

2000
A recovery complex of dormitories, clinic and office opens at Menagesha, funded by the Japanese Embassy in Addis Ababa

surgery. For him, Menagesha is the perfect location because it is close to Addis yet offers space and seclusion in a well-run, healthy environment. Like polio and fistula patients, those who have had noma operations return to their communities around the country. It's a mark of progress that, one way or another, they are accepted.

There will be other ways forward. This book is first and foremost a celebration of survival. The recent history of Ethiopia is at least as turbulent as any other country in the developing world. When Haile Selassie's family called on Leonard Cheshire to open a home in Addis Ababa it might have seemed that nothing could go wrong with such a well-connected venture. Little more than a decade later, Iskinder Desta had died in a Derg prison while Princess Seble was herself detained, along with her mother and sisters. Ethiopian genocide was punctuated by devastating famines in the 1970s and 1980s. Civil war (and the secession of Eritrea) marked the arrival of the 1990s. Today's Horn of Africa faces a multitude of challenges.

Somehow, the Cheshire organisation learned to cope. A symbol of its determination, begun 37 years ago in the first years of the Derg, is the annual fund-raising 21km walk. To start with, participants walked the highway from Addis to Menagesha. Now they follow a circular trail from the rehabilitation centre in striking countryside above the 3,000m (10,000 ft) contour.

For Cheshire, to walk symbolises freedom – and over the years many with polio have completed the 21km course. To walk also means garnering support from Ethiopian firms and individuals. Last November, Birr 574,080 ($32,360) was raised by the Menagesha walk, with parallel events in Hawassa and Dire Dawe. But it is more than symbolic or financial. Outside Addis Ababa and the urban centres, the principal way of getting between villages, to school or to market, is still by foot. With outreach services now embracing much of the country, CSE has improved life for many thousands of people and their families.

2001
Cheshire Homes is now Cheshire Services Ethiopia (CSE). Name-change reflects increasing focus on service-provision, with regional centre in Dire Dawa

October 2003
CSE establishes an integrated kindergarten at Harar, teaching disabled and non-disabled children

2004
Nahu-Senaye Araya becomes board chairman

May 2005
CSE rehabilitation centre at Hawassa opens improving outreach and other services in the south of the country

2006
Menagesha orthopaedic workshop renovation completed.
First riding project for disabled

2007
Prosthetics/orthosis outpatient clinic at Menagesha opens

October 2010
Reed House, CSE rehabilitation centre and head office, opens in Addis Ababa

February 2011
Facing Africa, the NGO tackling noma disease, opens its rehabilitation centre, the first in Africa, at Menagesha

Autumn 2012
CSE celebrates 50 years of Cheshire in Ethiopia

CHAPTER ONE

Miss T at home with the princesses

Cheshire's successful establishment in Addis Ababa was thanks to the Ethiopian royal family and an English SRN

On October 26 1935 Evelyn Waugh typed a short letter from Harar to his friend and confidante Lady Mary Lygon, who lived near Malvern, Worcestershire. He called her Blondy, she called him Bo. "I am sick to death of this country and these lousy blackamoors" he moaned. The budding novelist was on his way home after a stint in Addis Ababa covering the first Italian-Abyssinian war for the London Daily Mail. His experiences would be regurgitated in the comic masterpiece, *Scoop*.

Two years later, while working on *Scoop*, Waugh wrote to his brother Alec from Frome, Somerset, asking permission to amalgamate various family coats of arms to adorn his newly-acquired house. He was desperate to impress people. As it happens, just a few miles north in the city of Bath, the "blackamoor" emperor Haile Selassie was ensconced with his extended family after escaping from the same war. Selassie and his dynasty had an ancient aristocratic pedigree Waugh could never hope to match, for all his wit and connections.

Apart from the emperor himself, five members of the royal household then living at Fairfield, the rambling Bath mansion, are central to this story: Princess Tenagnework - Haile Selassie's oldest daughter, who in fact was born in Harar - and her children Iskinder (Alexander), Seble, Sophie and Ruth. Princess Tenagnework was the wife of Ras Desta Damtew, a well-born general in the Ethiopian army who stayed to fight the Italians. He was captured and executed by them towards the end of 1936. She, still only in her mid-twenties, ran the house in Bath for her father (her mother was mostly in Jerusalem); her six children (two sons, four daughters) were all under 10. As they became of school age they were educated in private institutions around the West Country.

Fast-forward 25 years. Early in 1961 Leonard Cheshire VC, the British war hero turned humanitarian whose selfless example in creating refuges for the sick and disabled was starting to resound around the world, received an invitation from two of Haile Selassie's grandchildren. Commander Iskinder Desta, who was to become head of the Ethiopian navy, and Princess Seble Desta requested he visit Addis Ababa to discuss creating a Cheshire home there.

Iskinder wrote to Cheshire: "As in all countries and especially in Asia and Africa, we have hundreds of crippled and sick children, mothers and fathers who are helpless and poverty stricken and who greatly need the assistance of such organisations as yours". He rather spoiled this humanitarian gesture by expressing, at a later date, sentiments that would not have sounded out of place in the mouth of a Victorian social reformer: "The real problem, of course, is that the disabled go round begging and are a nuisance in the city. There are some Homes that have been established for them, but they feel that begging is more profitable, so one of our difficulties will be in convincing the disabled that the Homes provided for them will not only help them materially but morally, with the emphasis on the moral side."

Ethiopia had hardly been among Cheshire's personal priorities. He'd already opened a home in Sierra Leone, but his heart lay in the infinite quandaries of India. However, when he visited Addis on the way back from a trip to India he was made a proposition he could hardly refuse: the royal family would find room for the home in one of their houses, would head up the local organising committee, and would co-opt the great and the good. Cheshire responded by sending out, in February 1962, one of his best young staff members, the State-registered nurse Denise Tabernacle. She brought with her just £50 and a five-year remit from head office.

Anglo-Ethiopian ties were strong. Allied success in chasing out Mussolini's forces in 1941, inspired by the opportunistic journalist George Steer and the messianic Major-General Orde Wingate, led to Italian colonial rule being exchanged for a looser-limbed but still restrictive British administration. Among those putting pressure on the authorities to reinstall Haile Selassie was Brigadier Dan Sandford, who had also played a key role in ousting the Italians and for whom Ethiopia was home. Sandford's daughter-in-law Pippa became a long-serving Cheshire board member. She was also head teacher of Sandford International School, created in the 1940s for the English-speaking community by Sandford's wife Christine.

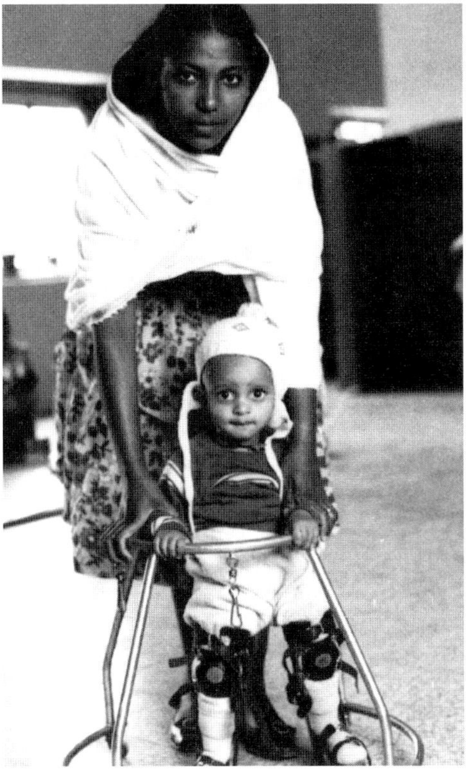

An early picture of a girl with her young sister, brought in for treatment. Children exercising on the mat were at the Asmara day centre opened in 1969

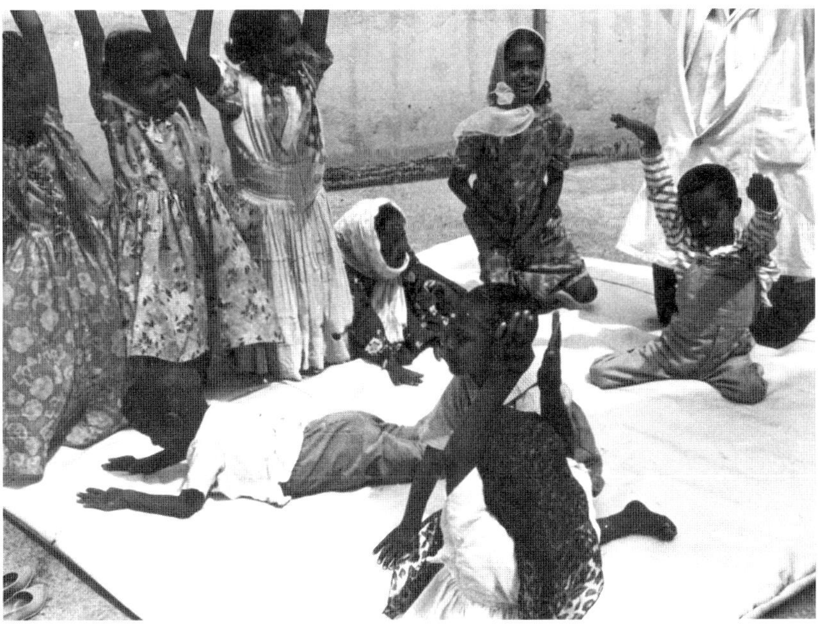

Because history brought them to England as children, Iskinder and his sisters grew up almost as British as Ethiopian. Iskinder's uncle, Prince Mekkonen, only a few years older than him, was educated at a Bath preparatory school and Wellington College. Iskinder himself was sent to prep school at King's College, Taunton. An Acme press photo of June 1938 has him in fine form on the grass running track there. The caption reads: "His dark legs flying, Prince Desta, grandson of Emperor Haile Selassie, is shown as he crosses the finishing line to win the 100-yards dash for boys under 10".

Iskinder also went on to Wellington, then to Dartmouth Royal Naval College and began his naval career as a midshipman on HMS Gambia (the same ship which had brought Haile Selassie from Malta to Portsmouth at the start of the emperor's state visit to Britain in October 1954). He was pictured in the April 5 1956 edition of JET, the American "weekly negro news magazine", on board HMS Gambia at Devonport. The princesses were sent to Clarendon School, a small independent girls academy originally in Malvern which transferred to North Wales. Princess Seble graduated from Oxford. Their generation, including Princess Ruth who also helped with Cheshire, was thoroughly modern, about as far away from Waugh's cleft-stick caricature as is possible.

All the same, their mother Princess Tenagnework was the driving force behind provision for Cheshire and, equally importantly, for the Fistula Hospital, established just before the revolution. The princess had a reputation for being highly conservative but with a strong sense of noblesse oblige. In an atmosphere of growing political and social unrest, as Haile Selassie declined to instigate much-needed reforms, Princess Tenagnework quietly demonstrated that she and her family cared.

The Cheshire Home for Retarded Children opened in half of Princess Sophie's Kasanchis house during 1962. The handful selected, just three at first but numbering seven by the end of November, were children with learning difficulties rather than physical disability. Some were to stay many years. It was no more than a gesture to wider problems, but Cheshire made an immediate mark in the diplomatic wives' community and soon muscled in on the Rotary Club, who provided equipment for an exercise room installed at the back of the house in July 1963, following a decision to admit the physically disabled as well. An association formed to support the project financially also provided its executive committee.

When the formidable Margot Mason, the Cheshire Foundation's

general secretary, visited in the autumn of 1963 she was impressed. She started her report in this way: "Miss Tabernacle has done, and is doing, a very good job. She has organised the little Home beautifully. There are 11 children at present with a further two coming this week. All are happy and well looked after...Miss Tabernacle gives them physio-therapy and teaches them to knit, weave etc. A teacher comes to give some of them lessons each morning but one or two of the older children go to school. The children sweep the floors, wash up their dishes after meals and make their beds. Miss T plays with them after tea and they have dancing and singing after supper before they go to bed."

Miss Mason's assessment of the Desta family was somewhat less generous: Princess Seble – "Deeply interested and keen that the Home should flourish. Rather too busy with other activities to be able to spare enough time, but at present she is the key to everything." Princess Sophie – "I did not meet her as she was away. I gather she goes along and plays with the children. She has lent her house and furniture for the Home." Princess Ruth – "at present away in America with the Emperor, but wishes to resign" (from the committee).

In an early annual report, Princess Seble herself paints a warm picture of the British administrator: "The Church of the Latter Day Saints and the English Church kindly presented a car which has been received with great enthusiasm and you may have seen Miss Tabernacle sitting up very straight in her vehicle on her way to do the children's shopping, with the children themselves grinning away in the back seat."

By that time, however, moving to Gefersa (Menagesha) was already the main topic of conversation. "Miss Tabernacle was very much against it for she said it was far out and that support for the Home was gained only by her own social contacts," Margot Mason observed. But Princess Sophie needed her house back. Ever the realist, Miss Mason concluded "As we depend for any Ethiopian support on the interest shown in this work by the Desta family I think we can hardly go against their wishes regarding the property."

Gefersa, a rural estate outside Addis on the Ambo road, had belonged to Abba Hanna, Haile Selassie's personal confessor who lost his life in the abortive palace coup of 1960. It was willed to Princess Tenagnework who offered it to Cheshire, and indeed the institution was known as the Abba Hanna Memorial Home. At the time Menagesha was inaugurated by the emperor with Leonard Cheshire in attendance on December 6 1965,

16 children had come under Denise Tabernacle's care. The full move there was not completed until a year later.

Despite the inconvenience of commuting the 27km between town and country there were obvious pluses in the sweet air and the peaceful environment. By then, half the young residents had physical disabilities and polio was recognised as the major challenge. The working relationship with physiotherapists and doctors at the Princess Tsehay Hospital had been led from the beginning by a Yugoslav doctor, Mira Evanovitch, herself a Cheshire committee member.

The late 1960s were again a time of change for Cheshire, signalled by the departure of "Miss T" in 1967. As numbers of children increased, priorities emerged. This led to the radical conclusion that Cheshire could not continue to offer purely residential care if it were to tackle the rash of new polio cases. The board of management, created early in 1968, decided within months to accept only physically disabled children and to start discharging rehabilitated children from Menagesha. This was the origin of the process which has allowed over 100 children a year to pass through the Menagesha rehabilitation centre.

At much the same time, the Cheshire Foundation in London responded to a call from Eritrea, then a province of Ethiopia, by opening a day clinic for polio patients in Asmara, working with local hospitals and also funded by Princess Tenagnework. In true Cheshire fashion, this successful initiative was quite independent of Addis Ababa and received no grant-aid from the Cheshire Foundation. Leonard Cheshire himself laid the foundation stone for a residential home at Asmara in 1973 which was never built - scuppered by political developments. The Asmara initiative had its own management committee and a volunteer physiotherapist.

There were parallel developments in Addis, where a weekly polio clinic was opened at the Ethio-Swedish Clinic run by Dr Nellie Dekker, a Dutch paediatrician with call on other hospital staff. Cheshire employed its first social worker to follow through with families often loth to accept children back home after operations, because disability was believed to be a curse from god.

When the social worker left he was replaced in November 1972 by Gebremedhin Bekele, who apart from a short break has been with Cheshire ever since and eventually became CSE's executive director. His personal achievement in holding the organisation together through four extremely testing decades cannot be overstated.

Denise Tabernacle, who established the home in Addis Ababa, seen at a social event. She's standing next to Leonard Cheshire

The 1970s had begun optimistically for Cheshire with a new residential block at Menagesha funded by Haile Selassie and opened by the emperor in 1972. This allowed for up to 80 children, much as today, and provided a clinic as well as domestic facilities. A volunteer British physiotherapist, Gillian Hall, became matron and ran the establishment with skill, charm and warmth.

Farming, always thought to have economic potential, was enthusiastically embraced, along with a market garden and more cows. Vegetables were sold to the Hilton and Ghion hotels and milk to the Shoa Dairy. But the expected profits did not materialise.

Education was an issue – children often attended the local Ethio-Yugoslav school – but so too were training opportunities in the rural surrounds. Significantly, a workshop to make orthopaedic appliances opened in 1972 not only provided better, cheaper leg braces, shoes and crutches than could be bought but offered training and work opportunities to disabled operatives.

Menagesha had been carefully established, was funded in a hand-to-mouth way and, although still dependent on volunteers, made a valuable contribution to the battle against polio. It was a solid start.

How RAF Khormaksar helped build Menagesha

A Blackburn Beverley flown by 83 Squadron Royal Air Force based at RAF Khormaksar, Aden, landed at the Old Airport, Addis Ababa, several times during 1965 on one of the nobler missions of empire. The transport plane had chugged across the Red Sea and up into the Ethiopian Highlands with cargos of building materials, items like a generator or a Land Rover, and many willing hands.

Given Leonard Cheshire VC's standing with the RAF and the backing the project had from the Ethiopian royal family it's hardly surprising that volunteers lined up in the messrooms of Khormaksar, and that work to modernise the site at Menagesha, which had been donated by Princess Tenagnework, was accomplished with smiles all round.

The biggest challenge for the organising committee in Addis Ababa was how to make the most of such wonderful PR opportunities without upsetting those who, month in, month out gave of their time for the home's welfare.

These historic RAF publicity photographs show work in progress (see page 11). They are also a charming record of Princess Tenagnework and her three daughters meeting RAF officers and men (see page 7), and a one-off chance to see the two principals, Emperor Haile Selassie and Group Captain Leonard Cheshire, inspecting the airmen – as well as each other.

Margot Mason, Cheshire Foundation's general secretary, had visited Aden on her way to Addis in October 1963. There she met Squadron Leader Reg Petch who was keen to help out in Ethiopia, while Flight Lieutenant Glen undertook to organise "adoption" of the first six children at £52 a year. They also showed interest in opening a branch of Cheshire in disused air force buildings at Sheikh Ottaman near to Khormaksar.

That came to nothing, and just two years later RAF Khormaksar closed as Britain retreated west of Aden. Soon the royal family would be facing major problems at home. Both empires were in trouble. But the flight of stone steps the RAF built up to what's now the Menagesha workshop is as solid today as it was in 1965.

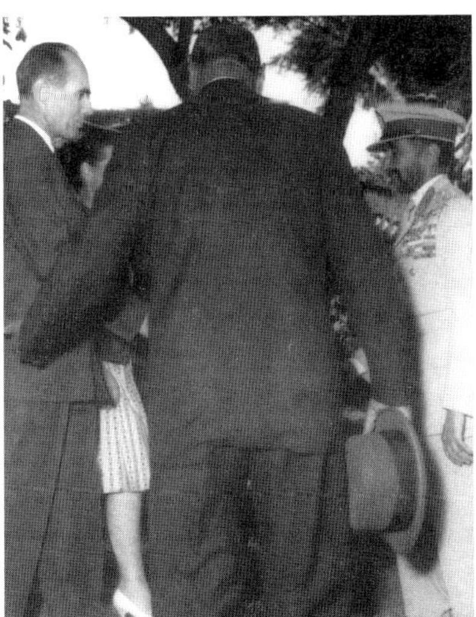

Men and equipment arriving at Addis Ababa airport. Leonard Cheshire's encounter that day with Haile Selassie was far more formal than Princess Tenagnework's handshakes with RAF volunteers. The two leaders also reviewed the helpers

Profits always a challenge for the Cheshire Home Farm

Menagesha's farming potential had been seen by the royal family as a way of financing the home. A 1966 report by P.D.Wood, one of the early British volunteers, describes how in December 1965 Princess Tenagnework donated five Friesian-Zebu milking cows for a cowshed built by another British volunteer, Nick Able.

They provided milk, produced two heifers and more were expected since the princess then sent a bull, immediately named Ato Nick. The report also mentions pigs and sheep to provide food for the children, two oxen to draw the plough and a vegetable garden producing surpluses sold in Addis.

The Cheshire Home Farm, as it was cleverly if cozily called, was at that stage costing more than it returned – a state which, despite huge efforts over the years, has hardly changed. Perhaps the ten hectares available for cultivation were never sufficient to be profitable without the sort of intensive farming methods alien to Cheshire's philosophy.

At about that time another British volunteer, Neil Walton, assumed responsibility for the farm. He writes of those days:

"I was a VSO agriculture worker at the Cheshire Home in the early 1970s. My predecessor had unfortunately died of gas poisoning whilst taking a bath after a long day on the farm. My job was to work with the existing local team to revive and diversify the farm enterprise in order to provide produce for the centre and income for its recurrent costs, as well as to help with the overall management and development together with Gillian Hall, the VSO physiotherapist I was lucky enough to work with.

"We struggled for a while with improvised technologies and 'seat of the pants' methods and eventually worked our way up to a brand new tractor and machinery, 15 Holstein in-calf heifers, new sheds and stores for animals and produce, and a super VW combi pick-up for marketing the vegetables from the large irrigated area.

"We claimed to be the first farm in Ethiopia to grow brussels sprouts on

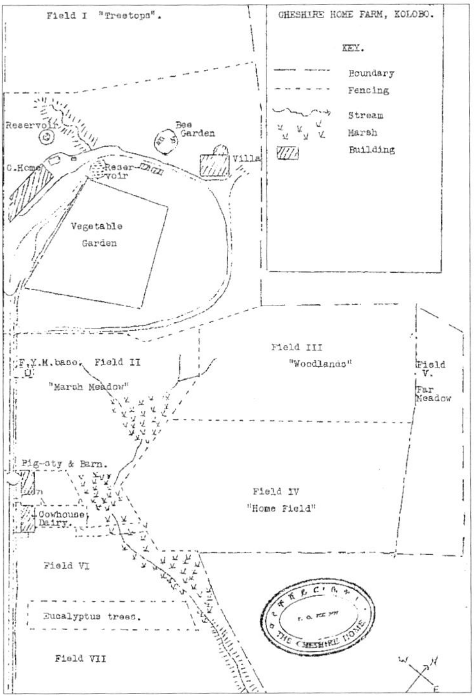

a commercial scale, which we sold at inflated prices to the hotels and new supermarkets in Addis.

"When the milk eventually began to flow we attempted to get a butter-making enterprise moving, but the children drank too much of the main ingredient, so we concentrated on egg production and the supermarkets had our Cheshire Home name stamped on each of our eggs they sold.

"We planted cereals where we didn't need grassland and put in new eucalyptus plantations. Despite the basic success of the business, the growth of the centre's activities and budget continued to outstrip the net income capacity of the farm and we had to complement this with other income generating ideas.

"We ran many fund-raising events including an annual bonfire, annual walk, home-made produce bazaars, dance evenings, open days, and anything else we could think of. Many friends of the centre put in a lot of energy and time to help with this. Our monthly newsletter was well received by supporters, who proved to be very loyal."

On balance the farm has been a distraction, though its presence and potential remains tantalising and there have been interesting experiments like producing biogas. In recent years the dairy herd was sold to provide core funding for the new rehabilitation centre at Dire Dawa. Horses offered by the British Embassy and stabled at Menagesha allowed children for a time to have riding lessons as part of mobility and confidence training. This offer may well be repeated.

Current plans to invest in the farm may finally make it a reliable source of income over and above providing nutritious organic food for Menagesha's children. But there are no guarantees.

'We have spent most of the year bedevilled by lack of money'

Cheshire struggled to survive without a guaranteed income from day one. The Annual Walk of 1975 was an inspired response to the Derg. It became an institution

From the time when the Home opened in part of Princess Sophie's Kasanchis house, with the backing on the Ethiopian Royal Family and the name of Group Captain Leonard Cheshire, most people have imagined it to be an unusually well-funded charity.

That was never the case. Of course, Emperor Haile Selassie, his daughter Princess Tenagnework and her own daughters, the princesses Seble, Sophie and Ruth, were in their own ways very generous to the Cheshire Home. But it was support in property, kind and connections as much as cash.

Denise Tabernacle's report to the monthly Cheshire Home executive committee on June 28 1966 was minuted as follows, showing the extent of her financial concerns:

1. *The British Community dance brought the Cheshire Home $1500*
2. *Christine Jones's Dancing programme - $434*
3. *Five Guineas – Mrs Humphrey from Aden who visited the Home*
4. *£10 – Mr Robinson, BBC man who made a film on the Home*
5. *Three bags teff, Princess Tenagnework; one bag teff Princess Sophie which "saw the Home through the latest crisis"*
6. *Bulgar wheat – Catholic Relief Service*
7. *Mattresses for all the children from Mrs Telefson*
8. *40 blankets – Mrs Puttman Carmer via the Dutch Red Cross*
9. *Italian Community – Senoras Barcini, Godfrey and Martinelli, $50/month for Stephanos. $300 for three months for the Home*
10. *Tomato chutney now being made from the unripe tomatoes and sold at $1.50/lb*
11. *Letter from Mr Kaboha of UNICEF stating he cannot help us but will refer us to the non governmental organisation section*

Leonard Cheshire lays the foundation stone, in November 1973, for a Cheshire residential home in Asmara which, because of the Derg revolution, was never built

The Treasurer's Report to the same meeting read: "In savings account - $7,700. Monthly donations would stabilise accounts"

Under Fund Raising, the following: "Fund raising event cancelled for July as there has been too much in the recent past." One assumes the secretary meant too many events, not too much money.

Three years later Lady Bromley, wife of the British Ambassador, presenting the annual report of the Household Committee, was minuted as saying "we have spent most of this year bedevilled by lack of money and most of our efforts have been spent in fund-raising – sometimes with success, sometimes not."

By 1973 the problem of monthly income had been partly addressed, but with increased costs the situation wasn't much better. A thorough if unsuccessful appeal to the Ethiopian authorities for money to pay Ethiopian staff read: "Financially we are constantly on the bread-line... Even though we are fortunate enough to have so many friends our guaranteed regular income does not cover half our monthly costs. A continuous pressure has to be kept up to make sure that the money required to run the Home keeps coming in. At present, as usual, we have enough money in the bank for only a few weeks' running costs." *Continued on page 30*

List of donations for the financial year 1972-73

Ten years after it was founded, the Cheshire Home for Physically Disabled Children depended not just on financial contributions but on everyday gifts in kind from Addis Ababa's caring community. This alphabetical list, reproduced in full, shows just how many people, and how much goodwill, was involved.

Mr G.T. Ackland – Handicraft magazines
Mrs D. Acqua – Jumpers
Addis Zemen – Articles
Wo Alexandra Yoseph – Books, jewellery, cloth remnants
Mr B Aliprano and friend – Medical supplies
American Women's Community – Magazines
American Women's Philanthropic Association – Blankets

Mrs E Asfaw – Jars, tins, books, cards
Wo Aster Assefa – Cot

Wo Belainesh Melete – Tin of oil
Dr Berhanu H.S.I Prize Trust – Oranges
Miss M Boucher – Clothes and radio
British Embassy – Free transport of goods
Mr E W M Bryant – Clothes

HE Mr A Campbell and family – Clothes and other items
Capuchian Franciscan Monks,
St Francis Friary – Service, film, sweets
Catholic Seminary – Play for children
Miss A Chamberlain – Clothes
Mr and Mrs J Coley – Men's suits
Rev and Mrs P Cousins – Books, Christmas gifts
Dr D Cox – Electric train set
Mr E Crook – Jars and tins
Mrs K Curtis – Books

Mr and Mrs J Dalton – Books
Dr P A Dekker – Clothes and other items
Mr W L Dekker and parishioners – Socks
Mr and Mrs F Diment – Clothes, toys, etc
Miss M Dion – Tapestry
S.M.Sgt and Mrs W D Dupir – 8mm projector

EELPA – Electricity at industrial rate
Wt Elfenesh Adane and friends – Books
Mr J Elford and Dr D Larsen – Books
Mr E Erzingatzian – Magazines
Ethiopian Airforce – Free transport of goods
Ethiopian Amalgamated PVT Co – IQ UREA fertiliser
Staff of Ethiopian Amalgamated – 1Q DAP fertiliser
Ethiopian Herald – Articles
Mrs E Exley – Fruit and clothes

Mrs Frenda – Books, crayons, clothes

Wo Genet Wolde Gabriel – Balloons and fruit
Ato George Aslandis – 4000 bricks
German Embassy personnel – Two rabbits and books
Girl Guides, Cyprus – Clothes

Jos Hansen and Soehne – Cough syrup
Mrs A Heffernan – Clothes
Wo Hirity Tedla – Wheelchair
Mrs Hobday – Clothes, toys, etc
HVA – Buses to and from Langano, sugar

Indian Embassy – Handloom
International Women's Club – Clothes

Jerry, Kenya Seed Co – Fertilizers, maize seed
Mr and Mrs G S Johnson – Books, records, decorations
Juventus Club – Cakes, biscuits, drinks

Mr V Karibian – Material, samples etc

Mrs Langenbacher – Clothes, table football
Mrs W Leah – Books
Mrs Leeman – Poem about the children
Mr D Leete – 4Q UREA, aphid spray, TSO
Wo Lemlem Tesfaye – Clothes
Mrs C Littlejohn and pupils of Princess Sophie's school – Clothes
Mr R Love – Free transport

Mr Macdonald – Books
Mr G Mackenzie – Iron, fan heater, desk set
Mann, Judd & Co – Free auditing of accounts
Mrs Mansfield – Clothes
Mr B Mansylla – Clothes, toys, other items
Mr G Marsden – Clothes
Professor Michael – Clothes
Mrs B Milaca – Clothes
Rev Miller – Books
Mrs and Mrs J Milne – Books
Mitchell, Cotts & Co – Free Land Rover repair, wood
Mrs G Morgan – Clothes
Mrs G Morris – Turkey, pies for Christmas

Mrs W Morris – Fruit, table tennis net and bats
Mr Mosin Fidali – Free projector repair, clothes
Mrs V Murray – Clothes

National Chemical Industries – Paints
Nativity Boys School – Clothes etc
Nativity Girls School – Party, blankets, clothes
Mrs J Need – Soft drinks, wine for Christmas
Mrs Niamir – Films at the Municipality

Mr Papadopoulos – Toys, clothes, sweets
Mrs Paradis – Blankets
Mr P V Patel – Clothes, fruit during Lent
Pegasus Cub Pack, Cyprus – Toys
Mr Perdiques – 6Q fertiliser
Mr K Pogharian – Stationery etc
Mrs B Pope – Clothes
Miss V Pow – Clothes, baskets, beads, etc

Mrs Renner – Clothes
Miss S Richards – Clothes, jars, tins, books
Ries Engineering – Inner tubes for Langano
Mrs Phyllis Ross – Jars, steam iron
Round Table – Party for the children, goodies

Mrs Sabetta – Clothes, sweets, etc
Ato Samuel Zewdie H Mariam – 16 litres V46 crop spray
Mrs P Sandford – Clothes
Mr Sandford's child – Toys etc
Mr and Mrs Schaerer – Clothes, sweets, presents
Dr and Mrs S C Scheer – Toys, clothes
Mr O N Scott – Ice cream maker
Mrs B Sevadjian – Sweets, biscuits
Miss S Sherbern – Books, clothes
Mr Singh – Books
Mr H Smith – Clothes
Mr Som – Toys, clothes
35 Squadron RAF Cyprus – Clothes, toys, blankets etc
Mrs A W B Strachan – Toys, clothes

HIH Princess Tenagnework – Turkey, Christmas puddings
Teklemariam family – 2Q teff, IQ beans, biscuits
Mrs F Thorne – Books
Wo Toyech Desta – Wheelchair
Mr and Mrs G Trefts – Curtains and chair
Ato Tsehay Woldelul and Mr S.F.Fernandes – Fruit

USAID – Vehicles, domestic appliances
US Embassy – Filing cabinet

Mr and Mrs Van der Meij – Clothes
Mr and Mrs H A Van Oerle – Clothes, toys, wheelchair
Varmdo-Skeppslags Rotary Club – Faffa
Mr and Mrs Vestin – International postage coupons

Mr and Mrs J Warrick – Clothes, toys
Wingate School – Children's books

Mr V Yohanssen – Clothes

Mr A Zecou – Monthly supplies of oil and soap
Wo Zenna – Books
Wo Zewdnish Lemma – Table tennis net, bat and balls

Cheshire's secretary also thanked "the many people who have contributed towards our fund-raising events during the year, including the Bonfire and Barbecue and the April dance"

Note: Addis Zemen was, and remains, an Amharic-language newspaper published by the government; fertilisers etc were donated for the Menagesha farm (Q=quintal); Lake Langano, south of Addis, is where children were taken for an annual holiday; teff and faffa are foodstuffs.

Continued from page 27. Despite such financial problems, Cheshire had been debating potential expansion plans before the Derg revolution of 1974. But with overseas volunteers no longer available, the royal family behind bars and a reduced international community, Cheshire's committee looked increasingly to itself for survival.

Its inspired response to the funding crisis was to create the annual Cheshire walk where people pledged sums of money for those completing the 21km course. Not only did this raise Cheshire's profile and spirits of a capital in deep depression, it also showed that the disabled were quite capable of making their own statements.

An unsigned report, discovered in the Cheshire UK archives, picks up the story of the first walk in 1975.

"Besides the annual Open Day, a ball at the Hilton Hotel in aid of the Home and organized by the Round Table (who also gave a Christmas party for the children at the Home), the Home pulled off its biggest fund-raising event in its history: a sponsored walk from the outskirts of the city to the Home itself – a distance of 21km – and it raised over Eth.$16,000 (approx US.$8,000).

"On the day, after all the publicity to find walkers and sponsors, 209 people set out and 199 walked the whole distance, including SIX of the children at the Home (one of whom was Bayenne, the Home's representative at the Cheshire Homes' International Family Day in England).

"The walkers started gathering at 9am and formed into groups of ten or so. Each group had a 'walk leader' who would stay behind with a walker who was unable to go any further until one of the three official cars came to pick up the exhausted person, and also to see that everyone in their group kept to the rules!

"The groups set off at an interval of five minutes and at three 'check-points' along the road they were able to stop for refreshments.

"Apart from a heavy shower in the afternoon which caught the latecomers it was a lovely day for a walk, and after the long rains all the Maskal flowers (yellow daisies) were in full bloom. Finally at the destination the Home provided all the walkers with a free meal and transport back to Addis Ababa."

As the illustration opposite shows, Mrs Joan Whalley, chairman of the fundraising committee for the second annual walk in October 1976, felt confident enough to write directly to the military government asking for permission, informing them that the government's own Social Committee had agreed to supply benzine and a military band!

የቸሻይር ቤት ለድኩማን ሕፃናት

THE CHESHIRE HOME
FOR
PHYSICALLY HANDICAPPED CHILDREN

ፖ.ሣ.ቁ. 3427 አዲስ አበባ
P.O. Box 3427 Addis Ababa

መሥራች፡ ግሩፕ ካፒቴን ቸሻይር፡ ቪ.ሲ. ዲ.ኤስ. ኦ. ዲ. ኤፍ.ሲ.
Founder: Group Captain Cheshire V. C., D. S. O., D. F. C.

ስልክ፡ መናገሻ፡ 4
Tel. Menagesha 4

Provisional Military Government
of Socialist Ethiopia
Ministry of Interior
Public Security Department
Addis Ababa.

13 September 1976

Dear Sirs,

The Board of the Cheshire Home for Physically Handicapped Children wish to hold another "Sponsored Walk" - a fund raising event which proved to be very popular and successful in 1975. To this end we should like to request the approval of your department, and the co-operation and assistance of the security police.

The Walk is planned for Sunday 31 October 1976, commencing at 9:00 a.m. and the route is from the A.L.E.R.T. Compound entrance (on the Jimma Road) to Meta Abo (Sebata) a distance of 20 klms. It is anticipated that between 200 and 250 walkers of all nationalities will participate.

We have contacted the Social Committee of the Dirg and they have very kindly agreed to supply us with benzine for the day and with a military band.

We look forward to your kind assistance in what we hope will be the biggest fund raising event for the Cheshire Home in 1976.

Yours sincerely,

Joan Whalley

(Mrs Joan Whalley)
Chairman of the Fund
Raising Committee

Mama Tsion, fashionista and counter-revolutionary

"I did voluntary work because there was nobody else to do it". Tsion Andom, known to all as Mama Tsion, became chairman of the Cheshire Home for Retarded Children after Princess Seble stepped down in 1965. She admits she didn't particularly want the job, which she held for less than a year, but when her friend the princess called she could not refuse.

At the time she was a successful fashion designer of well-born Eritrean descent, running a thriving business and very much part of the Addis and London scene. "I was always beautifully dressed in European clothes," she recalls, "everyone admired me. I made my own clothes, all my money went into clothes – my weakness. That's why I have no money. Now I wear the national dress. The dress I'm wearing is 50 years old".

Mama Tsion cuts a striking figure standing at the window of the bungalow which, she says, the Derg leader Mengistu Haile Mariam assigned to her when she was released from prison. One musn't be too precise about a woman's age, but as she heads towards her tenth decade Mama Tsion still drives a car and exudes vivacity.

The Communist revolution changed her life in a particularly personal way. Her closest brother was General Aman Michael Andom, a war hero and among the emperor's top brass when the Derg started to take over early in 1974. At first General Andom worked with the young Turks, becoming briefly chairman of the Derg. But he fell out with them on policy issues.

When asked to conduct the notorious purge of high-ranking officials in November 1974 the general refused, retreating to his Old Airport area house with a few loyal men and barricading himself in. He died that night in Mengistu's assault on the house. Tsion Andom, distraught, went round Addis openly criticising the regime – which imprisoned her from 1976 until 1990.

Today she lives amongst a photo-gallery of memories and with an undaunted ego. She tells the tale of sitting for the late Sir Gerald Kelly, celebrated for his portraits of the British royal family. "I love you. You are beautiful," Kelly said. The portrait sold recently for an undisclosed sum at London auction.

CHAPTER TWO

For Ethiopians faced with the Red Terror, fleeing wasn't an option

The 1974 Derg revolution brought tragedy to Cheshire's founders and proved a severe test to all who remained

"It was unbearable. Corpses were displayed at every street corner. Nobody knew what or who would be next. You were told you had to follow the Derg or die. I had a pistol levelled at my chest because I didn't seem to be guarding the revolution. Fleeing the country would have been best, but that wasn't an option."

Gebremedhin Bekele, Cheshire's social worker at the time, recalls the period in 1977-78 now known as the Red Terror, a consequence of the coup bringing the Derg and Mengistu Haile Mariam to power which started with a faltering government early in 1974.

The bad times began in earnest on September 12 that year when the emperor and most of the royal family were detained. Tragedy struck on November 23 when 60 top government officials, including Haile Selassie's grandson Commodore Iskinder Desta, were executed without trial in the Grand Palace.

The 2,700-year-old Solomonic dynasty, which had naturally seemed the guarantor of Cheshire's fragile little world, was suddenly its greatest liability. Not that anyone saw things that way at Menagesha, where news of the deaths and detainments left people numb. There was no alternative but to try to carry on as before, though the volunteers who ran Menagesha felt highly vulnerable.

Things only got worse as the Mengistu-stoked terror took control; among tragic events came the arrest and execution of Princess Seble's husband and father of five children, Lij Kassa Wolde-Mariam. He, Iskinder Desta and the emperor were representatives of Ethiopia at the funeral of US President John F Kennedy in November 1963.

Cheshire was patently providing a service the state did not, and despite the connections with the royal family it was recognised as apolitical.

That worked in its favour. According to Gebremedhin, "the Communist revolution restricted the activities of NGOs in the country. Most of them were nationalised but we escaped. We were open in all our dealings."

Events put pressure on historic links with the UK. As Sir Derek Day, British Ambassador from 1976-79, remembers, "Cool heads and patience were needed to cope with the hostility with which the British were viewed. The Cheshire Home in Ethiopia demonstrated these qualities. It went about its work calmly and effectively, ruffling as few feathers as it could."

Sir Derek adds: "The Home owes much to those Ethiopians who, at that time, ensured its survival through their energy and experience. A guiding force during our stay in Addis was Isaac Kifle, Cheshire's chairman, who fought hard and sometimes at personal risk."

Cheshire also had a stroke of luck. Not long before the revolution began, a trainee social worker had done a stint with the Home. As the Derg took shape, Captain Alamayu Haile became secretary-general of the Provisional Military Administrative Council. He was, in effect, number three in the Derg and proved a friend for Cheshire within the inner circles while he lasted.

From the start, nothing was easy. In May 1976, Gillian Hall, the physiotherapist who had been matron at Menagesha but had moved on to work at ALERT, the Addis hospital for leprosy patients, sent a report to Cheshire in London graphically describing problems at the rehabilitation centre:

"As you know things have not been going too well for a long time, and the last bout of trouble ended with Clare (the volunteer matron) leaving very suddenly. After this all seemed on the surface to settle down again. Lorraine (Lunden, another volunteer) went back out to the home and battled on. However, underneath the workers were forming together into a union. This is happening in every firm, hospital and institution in the country, not just Cheshire Home.

"Other things were happening too. Children were rebelling in many ways and giving Lorraine a really hard time. She and our social worker (Gebremedhin) eventually agreed to send several of the older children to a centre of the rehabilitation agency to get them out of the home and prevent them disturbing the whole peace of the home... The other children were very upset by the decision as they feel it's the home's duty to provide them with a home indefinitely (however badly they behave).

"Concerning the farm.... Last year it lost $3,000Eth (about US $1,500). So, after much discussion, the board finally decided to close it as a commercial enterprise. This meant laying off six workers, which caused a lot of anger. Two workers in particular got very angry and involved the Ministry of Labour. They together with Tadesse – the rehabilitation technician who makes the braces – got hold of the local Zemach students (used to spread the revolution in rural areas) and really stirred up trouble.

"Meetings followed meetings and eventually the labour committee of the board were supposed to go out to the house and sort things out. None of them could make it, so only Lorraine and Ato Isaac (Isaac Kifle) went. As they could not answer the union's demands satisfactorily they were locked up and held until the rest of the board should come out. Fortunately Ato Isaac's wife alerted the US Embassy... and riot police were sent out and rescued them the next day.

"Of course after this Lorraine and Neal Mabe (the manager) left the home and Mamo was given the responsibility of buying supplies as he is the only person at the home who can drive. This did not last long as Tadesse and the two Zemach students wanted to take over the home themselves. So this last week there have been more dramas as Mamo, Asrat, Adanech and Brhnau, four of our most dedicated workers, are in danger of being pushed out by the students. Numbers at the home are down to 45 as we are only discharging and not admitting under present circumstances...

"All these problems are basically political and are the result of the change of attitude running through the country. People no longer bow to authority easily, every move of those in authority is questioned. Every organisation in the country is having the same problems as Cheshire Home...I'm still hopeful things will work out. I still go out to the home regularly to treat the children and everything is still going on as ever."

Thanks to people like Gillian Hall, Menagesha did somehow work out, even though the protection afforded by Alameyu disappeared early in 1977 when he, along with seven others, was charged with plotting to eliminate so-called progressives in the Derg. They were summarily executed.

And there were narrow squeaks. Fr Colin Battell, Cheshire's chairman from the mid-1980s, recalls how Mengistu himself drove into Menagesha one day by chance on his way back from a trip. He liked the look of the place and was all for requisitioning it as a rest home for his bodyguard until he was persuaded by a delegation that Cheshire should be left alone.

In fact the 1980s would prove to be a time of expansion for Cheshire homes in Ethiopia. This expansion brought problems all of its own.

Shortly before the Derg revolution, in November 1973, Cheshire Homes held a regional conference in Addis Ababa, coinciding with a visit by Mother Theresa. At Menagesha she was shown round by the Cheshire Foundation's Ronald Travers and by Gillian Hall

Pillar of Menagesha

Although he has not officially worked there since the late 1970s, Mamo Eshete is one of the stalwarts of the centre

He was born there sometime before the Home was created. His father was the estate manager, reporting to Princess Tenagnework. As a youth he became handyman-driver for Denise Tabernacle, Cheshire's first administrator, who lived in Addis Ababa. One of his jobs was to follow up parents who had dropped off their children anonymously, attempting to be rid of them because they were disabled. "I didn't condemn them for that," he says.

Gebremedhin is the first to recognise his value, commenting "Mamo knows everything about this place". The two kept it going virtually double-handed through the worst days of the Derg.

At the April 19 1976 extraordinary board meeting after the chairman, Isaac Kifle, and one of the volunteers, had been temporarily held captive by "revolutionary" workers at Menagesha, Mamo was made de-facto manager of the home (Neal Mabe, the previous manager, had been ordered not to return there by the US Peace Corps). Mamo was also put in charge of taking sick children to the hospital.

The children's demands - including schooling to Grade 12, permanent residence at Menagesha, a union for handicapped children, and the dismissal of Gebremedhin - were all denied. Very slowly the home returned to a sort of normality, but without overseas volunteers.

Ethiopian staff had proved, in very difficult circumstances, that they could run the place. After the ex-pats' departure Mamo also found time to manage Menagesha's farm, something he'd done on and off during the 1960s.

When his contract expired in 1978, Mamo left to become a monkey hunter for taxidermists. Now retired, and like most Ethiopians without a pension, he's back working as supervisor at a local brick factory and still lives nearby. Unsurprisingly, he's often on hand to help out.

CHAPTER 3

Famine relief leads to an organisational split

Faced with the 1984 hunger crisis, Lady Ryder created Addis feeding centres which saved lives but spawned identity problems for Cheshire

The 1960s was a time of establishment and growth for Cheshire in Ethiopia; the 1970s saw regime-change which cut off the royal lifeline and sent most expatriate volunteers home; the 1980s proved to be just as turbulent, given the 1984 famine which set the eyes of the world on Ethiopia. This decade was also, paradoxically, a time of growth and diversity for the Cheshire brand.

Famine had, of course, been endemic in Ethiopia for decades. From the 1950s, spiralling population overtook and outflanked medieval farming practices. The number of heads to feed, estimated at 16 million in 1950, grew to 24 million in 1960 and 38 million in 1980.

Shocking scenes from Dessie, Wollo province, openly filmed by Jonathan Dimbleby for ITV's This Week in 1973 and transmitted as "The Unknown Famine", alerted the world to the dire conditions there. In a 2003 paper written for the Anglo-Ethiopian Society, Dimbleby claimed that UN agencies in Addis Ababa were well aware of conditions in Wollo but for political reasons had done nothing. He also accepted that a version of the film, doctored by Derg activists to juxtapose inserted images of the emperor feasting as thousands died of hunger and then broadcast widely across Ethiopia, was the trigger for revolution in February 1974.

The person who guided Dimbleby's researcher on his fact-finding first visit to Dessie was none other than Fr Kevin Doheny, a Catholic missionary working in Ethiopia for the Irish care agency Concern. Fr Kevin was to become Cheshire's Mr Africa, the man whose depth of local knowledge and contacts, as well as the confidence placed in him by Leonard Cheshire himself, coordinated Cheshire activities in African countries, including of course Ethiopia, during the late 1970s and the 1980s.

The Cheshire Home's work as an NGO coming to terms with polio in Ethiopia has never been headline-grabbing stuff. One of the problems in a country - as it was in 1980 - "locked" in military rule was that the day-to-day, month-to-month decisions had to be taken by a small group of expats and Ethiopians constantly looking after their shoulders.

The home's first organiser, Denise Tabernacle (who sadly died in September 1987) had made a return visit to Ethiopia in 1975. Her report back to London was typically perceptive: "It is high time, and I pointed it out to Isaac Kifle (the then chairman), that Ethiopians took over the running of the Home, especially as the whole political climate is changing and this continual change of volunteers is not good for continuity." Miss Tabernacle concluded with a nice cameo of expat existence: "The evening I arrived I was whisked off to a dance the Round Table were giving in aid of the Home (I had to make a speech and draw the raffle! What a laff!) and the place was packed in spite of curfews."

From Daniel Robel's 1987 academic paper, and from surviving board reports, one picks up the problems of the early 1980s. Robel put it this way: "Though the situation in the Home came back to normal in 1976 the Home did not show any significant development between the years 1976 to 1984. The Board, realising this weakness, formed an adhoc management committee at the July 1983 AGM".

As a result, consultants were engaged (one Ethiopian, one expat). Their report proposed strengthening the board and appointing an executive secretary to overcome the problem (which had existed in embryo ever since the move to Menagesha) of the committee being in Addis but the Home itself stuck away in the countryside, under managers of varying ability.

It wasn't just an internal challenge the board faced. Ethiopia was about to be overtaken by yet another crisis, the 1984-1985 famine in which up to a million people died. Not for the first time, Cheshire's local crusade against polio took a backseat. The difference from 1974 was that Leonard Cheshire's wife, Sue Ryder, together with the Cheshire Foundation's international director, Ronald Travers, visited Ethiopia in February 1985 with other things than polio in mind.

Baroness Ryder (she had been elevated in 1979) was a formidable woman whose humanitarian achievements matched those of her husband (he became Baron Cheshire only in 1991). Husband and wife, both Catholic converts, were deeply religious. Her natural response to the disaster happening before everyone's eyes in Ethiopia – and detailed so graphically in Michael Buerk's October 1984 BBC TV film – was to go to Addis and start something for herself.

The Cheshire Foundation's presence in Ethiopia was already complex. Apart from the Menagesha rehabilitation centre, an office in Addis and a day clinic at the Ethio-Swedish hospital, Leonard Cheshire had in 1969 established a day clinic for polio patients in Asmara (and laid the foundation stone for a residential centre which was never built). He had also come to agreements with Catholic establishments to create residential homes for mainly disabled children in regional centres at Gighessa and Asuela.

Wasting no time, Lady Ryder opened a feeding centre in Kebele 14, a very poor part of Addis. Of course, she could not do everything on her own. The Ethiopian who became her mainstay and the principal conduit of funding to Cheshire in Ethiopia was Negussie Wolde Selassie. Negussie, a person of great charm and ability, rose with such speed in the Cheshire hierarchy that by 1986 he was listed at the head not only of the new projects but also the original ones, throughout the country.

A separate Ryder-Cheshire committee was formed during the visit of Lady Ryder and Ronald Travers. Travers described conditions in Kebele 14, where they were taken by Negussie. "About 20,000 people are making use of one tap. There are no lavatories. Defecation is all around wherever you walk. There is abject poverty. People in rags and totally undernourished and underfed, living in conditions that defy comprehension." He noted that the food was provided by the Catholic Relief Service but administered and distributed by the Ryder-Cheshire Foundation.

It was crucial work, if not exactly what Cheshire had been set up to do. Ryder-Cheshire's local partner was stated as the Ethiopian National Children's Commission (NCC), and by August 1985 the feeding programme had extended to six neighbouring kebeles, along with provision of clean water taps and latrines. The focus was on children, and the aim was to establish a rehabilitation home for disabled youth in Addis at Mekanissa. Quite how that tied in with Menagesha was not spelt out.

In June 1986, the NCC held a conference chaired by Getachew Gebre to bring together representatives of the various Cheshire branches, in the

Committee members of the Ethiopian National Children's Commission in 1987. Pippa Sandford is flanked by Tessera Work Shimelis, in the blue suit, and Getachew Gebre. Gebremedhin Bekele is on the far left

words of Negussie, to "lay the foundation stone of unity and coordination." The NCC's deputy commissioner, Tessera Work Shimelis, in a keynote speech, noted that his government had accepted "the magnitude of the problem on the one hand and the hardly available services on the other."

Problems there were. But the amalgamation never really worked. The various homes had little in common, and shared even less with the feeding programmes.

Two years later, in April 1988, both Leonard Cheshire and Lady Ryder visited Ethiopia. Cheshire was returning from a long tour of homes in Southern Africa. They met up in Addis, where together they visited Menagesha as well as the Kebele 14 feeding centre, along with Ronald Travers. But at a meeting with the NCC, where Tessera was by then the commissioner, they were told of concern felt by the authorities about the confusion caused by the two bodies – the Cheshire Foundation and the Ryder Foundation.

The founders then held meetings with Travers and Fr Kevin at which it was agreed that the renamed Ryder Foundation Ethiopia would concentrate on community development work alongside the NCC, and on the feeding/water/latrine projects in Kebele 14. The renamed Cheshire Foundation Ethiopia (whose coordinating committee was to be called The Ethiopian Association of Cheshire Homes) would focus on Menagesha, with Mekanissa envisaged to work in tandem as a day/residential training centre for disabled teenagers. Official separation between the two foundations was formally agreed with the Ministry of Labour and Social Affairs.

Travers' May 1988 report also noted that Menagesha was functioning at only half capacity (35 children with room for 71) but pointed out that just one bed at the Ethio-Swedish Hospital had been allocated to Menagesha, so surgical operations were "extremely restricted." Out at Menagesha itself, money raised in memory of Denise Tabernacle was being used to build a staff house for volunteer expat physiotherapists in the hope that they could be persuaded to brave the country's difficult political climate.

Tellingly, Travers expressed worries about Menagesha, "for some years now I have not found this to be a happy Home," although he praised Rev Colin Battell (then Vicar of Addis) who, as chairman, "has done a remarkable job in the last two years." At the same time he commented that the Ryder-Cheshire feeding centre "is a great success, due to Negussie's immense hard work... VIPs visiting Addis are taken to see it, which shows how highly the authorities think of it."

So between 1985 and 1988, with Ethiopia still under the Derg and struggling to assimilate the knock-on effects of devastating famine, with national security an issue and Eritrea beginning to go its own way, Cheshire's presence in the country was stretched in all directions. Attempts to unify activities had not succeeded and the core fight against polio had not prospered (although 1988 saw the start of mass vaccination). While the decline of the Soviet Union left the Derg without a banker and Ethiopian liberation movements gained momentum, Cheshire simply struggled on.

Luckily, recurring pressures to move the rehabilitation centre from Menagesha had been resisted. Whatever organisational challenges it posed, the estate donated by Princess Tenagnework in 1965 was to prove Cheshire's indispensable base as Ethiopia moved towards more optimistic times during the 1990s, and services for the disabled started to grow in number and quality.

CHAPTER FOUR

Moving into today's world with an accent on service provision

Outreach and community-based activities have complemented Menagesha's role during the last two decades. The early 1990s were years of more change in Ethiopia as the two principal regional rebel forces which had ousted the Derg and forced Mengistu to find refuge in Zimbabwe established the Ethiopian Peoples' Revolutionary Democratic Front (ERPDF) provisional government. By 1994 this had settled into the Federal Democratic Republic of Ethiopia, a system devolving certain powers to nine regional governments under the overall leadership of today's prime minister, Meles Zenawi.

For Cheshire, this was a time of modest but significant gains. The first strands of the outreach service which today covers much of the country were set out from 1987, with teams visiting the Attat hospital, invited by the Catholic sisters there. Then, in 1994, funding from the Christoffel Blinden Mission allowed the management board in Addis to begin a programme of community-based rehabilitation under which the families of child beneficiaries were helped by social work teams. Cheshire was on the move, though Menagesha remained, as now, the operations centre.

As these processes started to take shape, Cheshire increasingly employed trained Ethiopian physiotherapists, social workers and technicians. The principal funding came from abroad, but the professional infrastructure no longer relied on expatriates. Having survived the Derg intact, Cheshire was one of the very few local NGOs able to propel itself into the modern era.

At the same time internal friction within the Cheshire organisation threatened to dilute efforts. The events of the 1980s, described in the previous chapter, meant that although the Cheshire Menagesha Home remained the centre of activities, all fund-raising and contact with the Cheshire Foundation in London - as well as coordination of other homes bearing the Cheshire name in Ethiopia - was managed by Negussie Wolde Selassie, the man brought in by Ryder-Cheshire. *Continued on page 48*

"There's no such thing as an orphan in Ethiopia"

Cheshire's chairman from 1986-94 stood his ground for Menagesha at a time when the Cheshire brand was diversifying rapidly

Today Father Colin Battell is a Benedictine monk, until recently Prior of Ampleforth Abbey in North Yorkshire. Twenty-five years or so ago, as Anglican Vicar of Addis, he became chairman of the Cheshire Home board. His tenure covered the difficult final years of the Derg and early years of the Meles regime. It was also a testing time for Cheshire's internal relationships.

Fr Colin was among the band Church of England priests who transferred to the Catholic Church at the time of the Anglican ordination of women priests. By then he was safely back in the UK, but much of his heart will always remain in Ethiopia. He's an Amharic speaker and an authority on the Ethiopian Orthodox Church. That, indeed, was one of the reasons he was originally posted to Addis.

He'd been involved with Cheshire for a decade before he succeeded Mekuria Tafessa as chairman. Perhaps his major achievement while chairman was in diplomatically standing up for Menagesha at a time when the Cheshire Foundation, represented by Fr Kevin Doheny and with Negussie Wold Selassie in place as Ethiopian organiser, wished to make it simply one of many homes in the country.

"The relationship with Leonard Cheshire was not straightforward," he remembers. "He was a very saintly man. But the attempt to bring different parts of Cheshire under one umbrella never worked. Nobody wanted it." He recalls the visit of Cheshire and Lady Sue Ryder to Addis in 1988 (see page 43). "Cheshire was very helpful. His wife was something else... The only time she smiled was at the camera."

Because he retained the respect of people like Ronald Travers, Cheshire Foundation's international director, Fr Colin managed to help keep

Menagesha independent. It was during his tenure that the crucial mobile outreach programme started, principally by coordination with Catholic missions in outlying areas.

He admires, in a humorous way, the ability of fellow men of the cloth to find funding for their projects and quotes the example of the home at Assela, run by Italian priests, then part of the Cheshire Foundation network but also well-supported from Italy. "They changed notepaper depending on who they were asking to donate."

Fr Colin was a great supporter of the rehabilitation routines under which most children stayed a maximum nine months. "Children in residential homes are seen as privileged, but we thought them much better off in the community. Once institutionalised it's very difficult to get rid of them. And there's no such thing as an orphan in Ethiopia."

Continued from page 45. Matters came to a head in 1996 when it was discovered that only a small percentage of funds from UK donors percolated through to Menagesha. Following a trip to see for himself, Alec (now Sir Alec) Reed switched the focus of support by his Ethiopiaid organisation to Menagesha. Eventually Negussie left for the US to join his wife.

The Cheshire Foundation (now Leonard Cheshire Disability) continues to support from London and Nairobi programmes run by the Cheshire Foundation Ethiopia (CFE) in Bahir Dar, Jimma and Dessie. This is an entirely separate organisation, a local NGO involved in community-based projects, with whom Gebremedhin Bekele and his team in Addis Ababa have cordial professional relations.

Jayne Shanyisa Muema, LCD's regional representative for the East and North African Region based in Nairobi, states that LCD sent a consultant to Addis in 2004 to help with CBR training and other capacity building.

"We capitalise on every opportunity to build the capacity of all our Cheshire partners, including CSE" she writes. "CSE is already doing such a great job and has proved that Cheshire partners can manage their own projects effectively...We cite them as a success story of how strong they have grown and the tremendous work they are doing in Ethiopia on disability."

Partly to help define its public profile, partly to reflect evolving practises, Cheshire changed its name in 2001 to Cheshire Services Ethiopia (CSE). Service delivery, as opposed to institutional care, had in fact been the case for many years, but the new name served to reinforce the brand. Under the chairmanship of Fr Colin Battell (1986-1994), Yehualshet Lemma (1994-1996) Lilla Heaslip (1996-2004) and now Nahu-Senaye Araya, the Menagesha board has pursued strong policies, adapted to the changing Ethiopian environment. It has opened up channels of working with the local, regional and national authorities which give it both responsibility and status.

Descriptions of CSE's main operational areas in the following pages attest the success of its approach in a country where there are few services for the physically disabled. As a role model for other local NGOs, Cheshire demonstrates that, on a relatively small budget, tangible results in essential operational fields can be achieved year on year.

Children fashion new lives in a secure, healing environment

In 2011 the physiotherapy unit at Menagesha Rehabilitation Centre treated 5,035 cases of people with disabilities ranging from post-polio paralysis to club feet, amputees, congenital deformities and cerebral palsy. Most, but not all, were children. The aim in each instance was to return the patient to his or her community better equipped physically, mentally and emotionally to deal with everyday life.

In some cases it will be a child's first taste of real life because their family or guardian may well have kept them hidden away out of shame, regret or even superstitious fear.

So the very fact of getting to Menagesha is an important moment in itself. Beyond the weekly routine of two children being prepared for surgery every Friday morning before being taken to the Balcha Memorial Hospital in Addis Ababa in the Cheshire Services Ethiopia ambulance, and returning to the countryside on the following Monday morning, is an organisation premised on self-expression and personal development.

Far from confining patients to invalid status, children are encouraged to think for themselves about the opportunities their new condition offers. Although physical therapy, schooling, learning new crafts and so on are important elements structuring the week, one suspects that it's the informal friend-making, talking, games of football or table tennis, or simply hanging out in the sunshine which is the most important factor of the child's five-eight month stay.

In fact, such a period is perfect for understanding their new selves. If it were a matter of weeks there would be no time to acclimatise; if it were years there would be the danger of boredom and institutionalisation.

Daniel Beyissa, CSE's project officer who manages Menagesha and lives on site, spells out the routine. After operations children spend a week in the recovery section while their wounds heal. Then plaster of paris is applied to stretch muscles, and the rehabilitation process begins. When, perhaps five months later, the time comes for the casing to be removed, the patient is measured for the caliper which will enable them to walk on their own two feet, often for the very first time. Then back to physio for exercising and gait training.

Before anyone is sent home the rehab team assess whether everything possible has been done in each individual case. Very occasionally they have to admit failure and perhaps extend the stay to eight months, by which time most are more than ready to leave.

Life at Menagesha could be the first time a child has enjoyed regular meals, a proper bed to sleep in and the chance to learn in a classroom. Don't they attempt to hang on to this, and put off going home? No, says Daniel, they usually want to get back to their own community – they're eager to show friends and family what they can do.

Children are discharged along with a counselling package. Parents or guardians must accept that they are no longer disabled. Usually it's not that difficult to change parents' perspectives when they see the difference in their children. Then they can be accepted as full family members, sent to school and expected to undertake family tasks.

All-round progress is monitored every six months. The regional centres in Hawassa, Harar and Dire Dawa, and the outreach teams which tour remote rural areas, (see pages 60-64) play a key role in this process. "Most of our cases are success stories," Daniel claims.

He believes that attitudes towards disability in Ethiopian society are finally changing for the better. Before, disabled children, particularly in rural areas and especially girls, were often hidden away. Of the 70 short-term Menagesha residents, 55 were typically boys. Today, there are usually more than 40 girls at any one time.

Another indicator – related to the success of outreach, and of the community-based activities in regional centres – is that Menagesha is heavily booked, despite the fact that there are now fewer new cases of polio in Ethiopia.

The age limit for accepting patients has been raised from 16 to 18 in an attempt to clear the backlog of post-polio paralysis cases (after age 18 the chances of successful muscle correction diminish steeply). Today polio cases account for under half of all those treated.

Accepting near-adults has brought new factors into play, but on the whole – according to Daniel – has not caused particular problems.

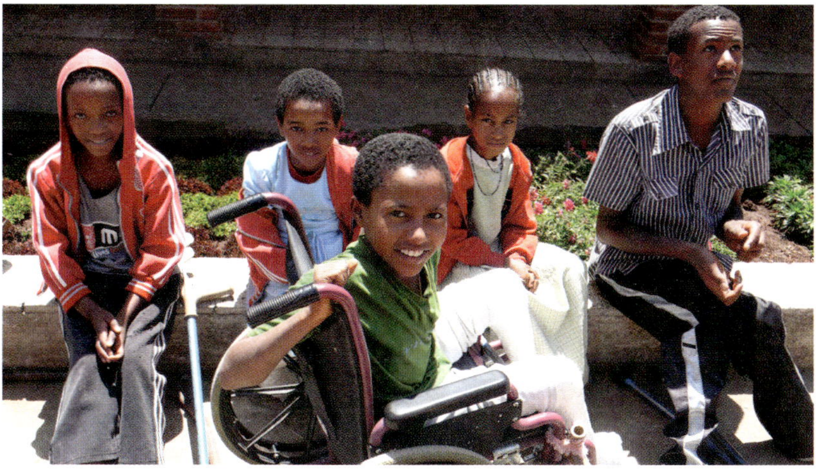

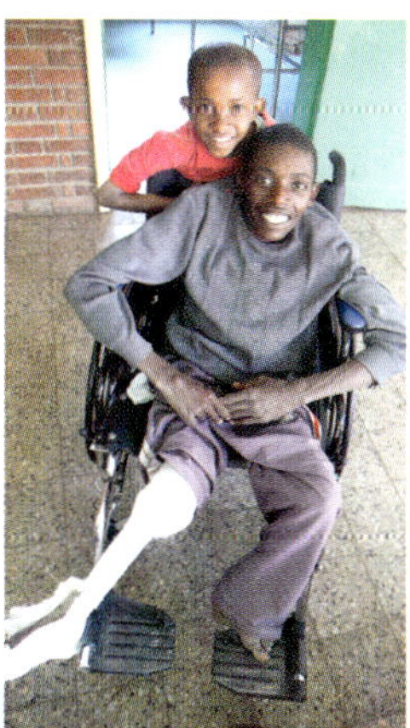

An essential part of rehabilitation at Menagesha is the time young people spend together, making friends and coming to terms with their new lives

"In any setting you will have misunderstandings. When we face aggression we allow the person to let off steam, then make him or her part of the discussion. When we sense issues arising we ask children to talk about them. We spell out what the boundaries are. We stress that they are here for rehabilitation, nothing else, and that they will soon be on their way."

Perhaps the strongest feeling expressed by children at Menagesha is that they see themselves, maybe for the first time, as individuals, focusing on their future lives. They answer questions politely, or nod permission to take photographs, but their real interest lies in discussion amongst themselves, in small informal groups. They come from almost every part of a huge country with very different ethnic, linguistic and religious backgrounds, but here they're part of a small, privileged group united by their transitional state.

This applies, too, to noma patients, who now have their own residential centre at Menagesha. In fact, before it opened, noma patients were housed in the main blocks and – despite the illness's dramatic physical nature – integrated with other children without problems. Mixing was encouraged by weekly events like a talent-spotting competition where those who choose to take part dance, sing, or recite stories – whatever they do best.

"When I first saw the noma children I was a bit shocked," Daniel admits, "but it didn't take me much time to understand." If processes and timescales are different, the essentials are the same. Children leaving Menagesha after treatment look and feel much better than when they arrived. Integration also happens in organised activities. And if the noma children prefer to shelter from the wider community that's their personal decision.

A measure of Menagesha's confidence is its stance on religion. In a country where most people are either practising Christians (primarily Orthodox) or Muslims, the centre is decidedly non-partisan. Observance is kept down to a moment of silence before a meal when people think their own thoughts. No religious opt-outs are allowed over food. Everyone eats the wholesome home-grown or home-reared produce.

Individuality is of course respected, but the key to complex organisation lies in keeping the processes continually on the move. "If the centre were to stop for one day the whole operation would be jeopardised," Daniel admits.

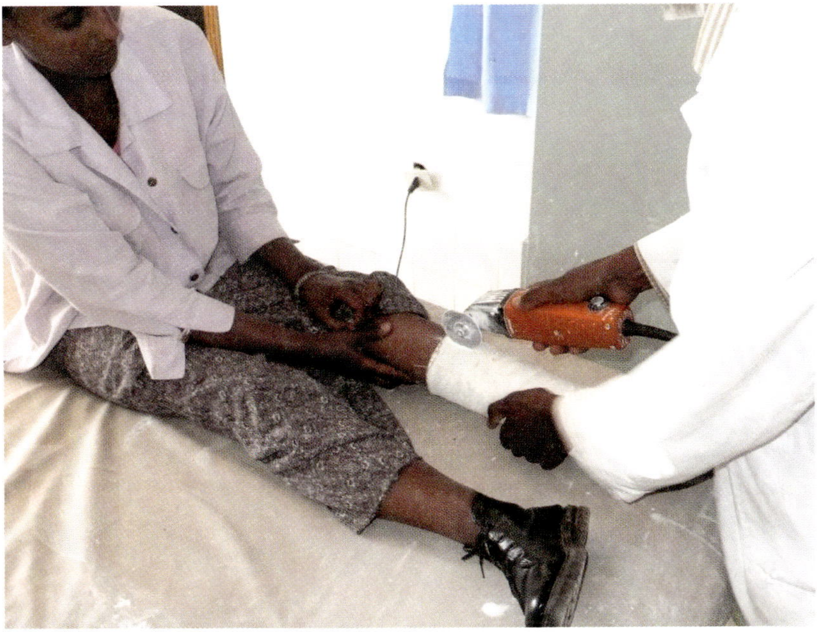

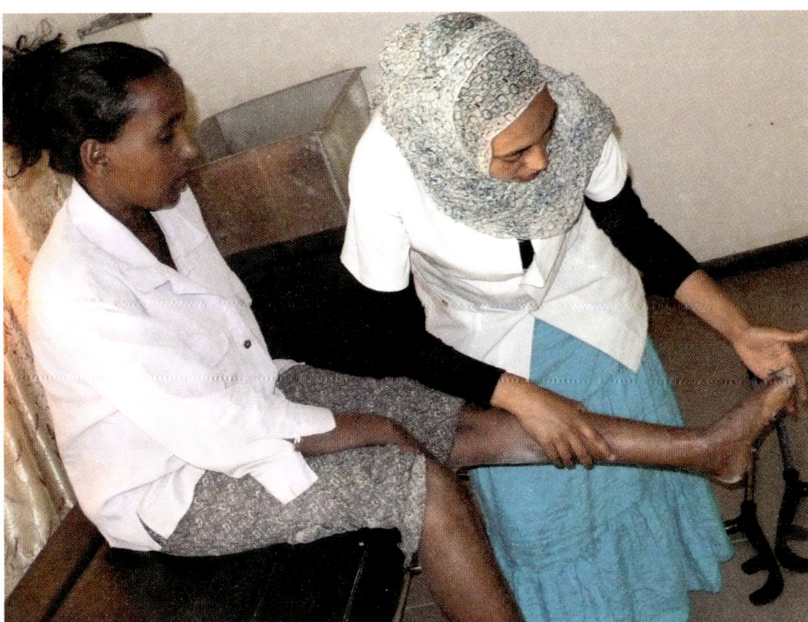

With post-polio patients, plaster of paris is typically applied for several months after an operation. The moment it is removed by a physiotherapist can be anxious, but then comes measuring up for an appliance and relative freedom

Balcha Memorial Hospital, the Russian connection

For the best part of 20 years surgeons at the Russian Red Cross Balcha Memorial Hospital in Addis Ababa have operated on patients brought by CSE from Menagesha, mostly post-polio cases. Two patients arrive on a Friday and leave on a Monday, week in, week out. Operations usually take about an hour.

Cheshire had previously used the government Black Lion Hospital, but switched after registering a high number of complications. The Balcha arrangement seems to suit both sides well.

Dr Evgeny Romanovskiy, chief of the hospital's surgical department, and his team of Russian surgeons, clearly see their Addis mission in humanitarian terms. Top staff stay there at least five or six years. The hospital was built in 1946 around a garden in the Lideta district, but Russian Red Cross medical involvement with Ethiopia goes back to the nineteenth century.

Dr Romanovskiy points out that traumatology is a Russian expertise, and that the hospital serves as a last resort facility for road accidents, of which there are a growing number in Addis. The service provided by the Russian Red Cross is not a money-spinner, though they do try to balance their books (CSE pays an agreed contribution towards its operations). Priests from the Ethiopian Orthodox Church receive free treatment.

Post-polio paralysis operations, involving soft tissue resection, are hardly the most complicated the surgeons will face. But Dr Romanovskiy and his colleagues are clearly happy with the fact that, between them and CSE, thousands of disabled children have been put on their way back to a productive life.

As the balance of patients moves away from post-polio to those with club feet and hereditary deformities the Russian surgeons look forward to new challenges from Menagesha, which they visit every now and then armed with presents.

They have also met the British surgeons who fly in with Facing Africa to operate on noma patients, and have the highest respect for them.

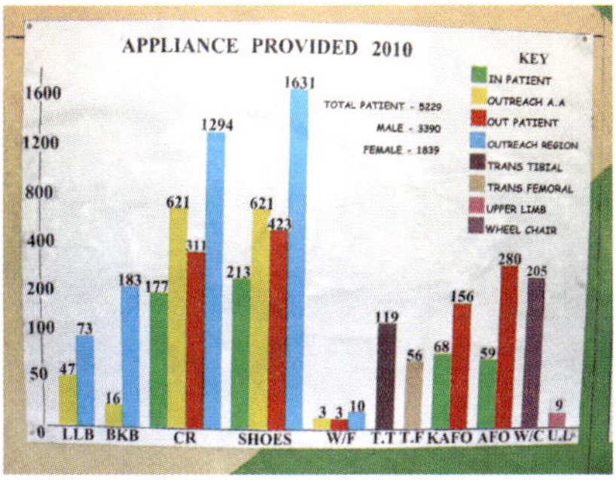

The wall chart in the Menagesha workshop shows how appliances made there in 2010 served 5,229 patients in all – as well as the split between sex, region and type of fitting. The workshop manufactures and assembles a complete range of orthopaedic devices. CSE's light-weight hand-propelled tricycle is also assembled there to individual specification

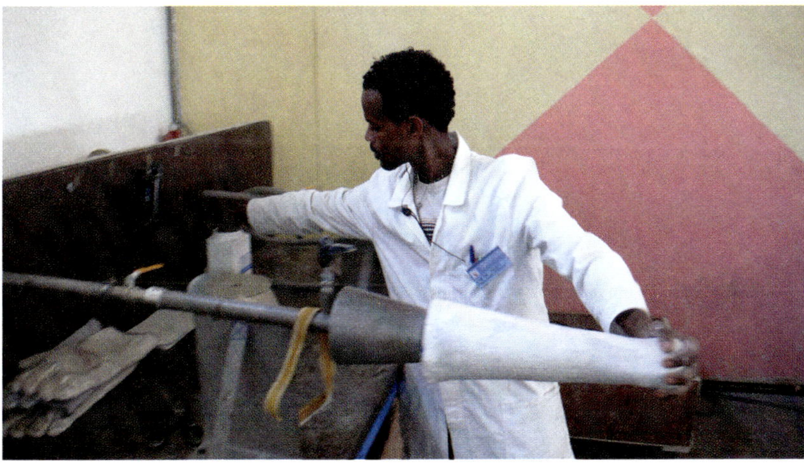

Disability, a challenge for everyone in the nearby area

Cheshire's approach to disability is that it neither starts nor ends with an individual. Many disabled people in Ethiopia have either a condition which could have been prevented by vaccination, or by better primary medical care. They are the product of an impoverished and backward society.

The environment which breeds them is also their home. When a person returns to his or her locality life must continue, but not as before. It's seen as vital that the rehabilitation achieved at Menagesha should not be allowed to slip away. Equally, the child's parents or guardians may well need support in their new role with, for instance, provision of a special toilet or school books.

That's the start of CSE's involvement in what's called community-based rehabilitation, or CBR. Projects in the Addis Ababa area, in Hawassa, Harar and Dire Dawa have taken rehab initiatives not just to the parents and siblings of disabled children, but into their communities via teams of young field workers.

They visit schools, talking to teachers about attitudes to disability and the fact that cross-disability is often related to one major problem. They attempt to make parents understand that disability is not a curse from God, and bears no shame.

They work with kebele (local area) and woreda (district) authorities – as well as with donors like Christofel Blinden Mission and Light for the World – to establish and spell out a programme for each child. After diagnosis, CSE's social worker sits down with the mother; together they make an agreement, a plan, which the mother signs. The message is "yes, Cheshire is here to help you but the prime responsibility is yours."

Life skills learned at Menagesha are passed on to parents. The assumption is that a typical family will be unlikely ever to see a doctor when it matters. So field workers teach so-called saliva techniques, low-tech solutions like the use of honey or other natural medicines to alleviate sickness and pain, together with first aid and practical hygiene.

CSE may decide to loan families small sums – from Birr 500-2,000 ($30-120) – and refer them to credit-givers, micro-finance organisations, which, working with the local authorities, often provide basic space in which to organise small businesses. These loans have to be repaid – and the percentage of people who default is low.

Of course, when families have to contend daily with open sewers, communal latrines and the absence of safe drinking water – let alone water in which to wash clothes or pots and pans – rehabilitation is often an uphill struggle.

If CSE cannot by itself cure deeper malaise it can demonstrate that simple procedures go a long way to helping people help themselves. In working alongside officials from the kebeles and woredas it also ties effectively into the Millennium Development Goals which Ethiopia fully endorses but is struggling to meet by 2015.

Housing conditions for many are basic throughout Ethiopia's urban areas

For amputees, a route back to normality

Behind Menagesha's visitor reception area, close to the car park, the out-patient department treats a different category of disabled. Normally adults, typically amputees, they come from all over Ethiopia for free measurement and fitting of prosthetics.

They stay between 15 and 20 days while the limbs are made in the CSE workshops, living in local communities nearby. The cost of their stay is covered by CSE, which both makes it easier for outpatients and fosters good relations in the Menagesha area.

Patients come via an appointment system, on a four or five month waiting list. They must get themselves to the centre, but the return bus trip is paid for. Every year about 1,500 people are seen in this way.

Kebede Geresu and Habtamu Tassew, seen opposite, are amputees who visited the centre at the same time in March 2012, becoming friends. Kebede lost his right leg after gangrene set in following a motorcycle accident. Habtamu also lost his right leg to gangrene while in hospital being treated for pains in the leg.

When photographed, Kebede was feeling his way with the new prosthetic, Habtamu was about to be fitted. They were in high spirits at the prospect of returning home, and both seemed very satisfied with the treatment received.

Kebede, a male nurse himself, was all set to hand out CSE's details to other disabled people, and no doubt to ride a motorcycle to work again sporting his new leg.

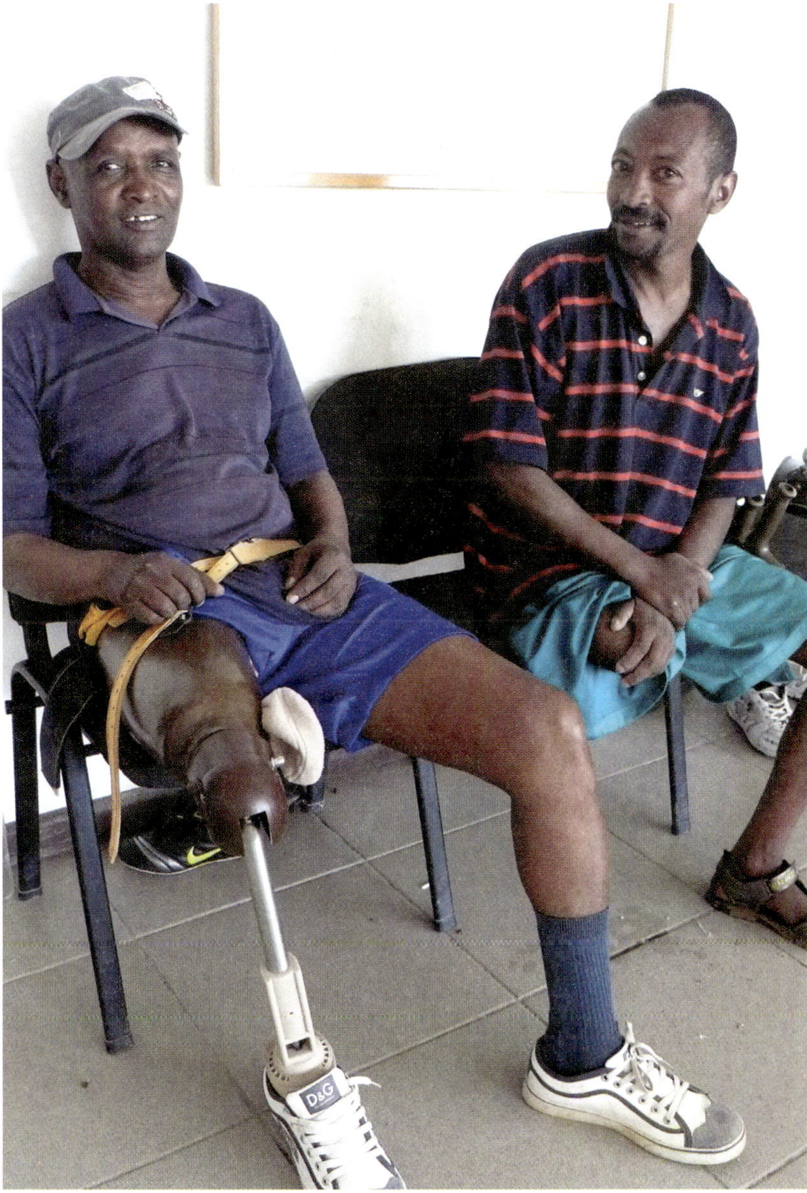

Kebede Geresu and Habtamu Tassew at the Menagesha outpatient clinic

Outreach bus a lifeline to remote rural areas

The woreda, or local authority area, of Jimagenet is about 360km west of Addis Ababa towards the border with South Sudan. Half of this distance is covered by a modern tarmac road which passes through the pleasant resort town of Ambo. At Gedo, where the tarmac runs out, there's a choice between carrying on along the main highway towards Nekemte - and looping continuously around construction stretches as a purposeful Chinese-led outfit engineers a new alignment - or branching off on the longer but complete dirt road to Shambu.

Either way, the journey takes around eight hours in a powerful 4x4 land cruiser. The converted bus belonging to Cheshire Services Ethiopia, which serves as a mobile workshop for the outreach team of four, will need 12 or 14 hours to cover the distance. It's a gruelling drive, but by no means the furthest destination from Menagesha where the team is based.

Having spent two long days at Jimagenet seeing a variety of cases, the bus moves on to Sibu Sire (half a day's travel) where the team works just one day, then off to nearby Konche for two days before transferring to Gida Ayana for three working days and Nekemte for another three days or so.

By the time the bus returns to Menagesha the team will have been away from base for 18 days and having covered 1,182 km. Some 284 clients will have been examined, assessed and either supplied with new/altered appliances or referred for appropriate services, perhaps hospital operations and Menagesha rehabilitation.

Geographical centres served have few medical facilities, and certainly nothing in terms of orthopedic treatment. Sometimes there's no nearby hotel, and if there is it will offer very basic comforts. The team, comprising a physiotherapist, two technicians and driver who also doubles as a technician, are used to fending for themselves. Nothing surprises them (some teams include a social worker, depending on need at outreach points).

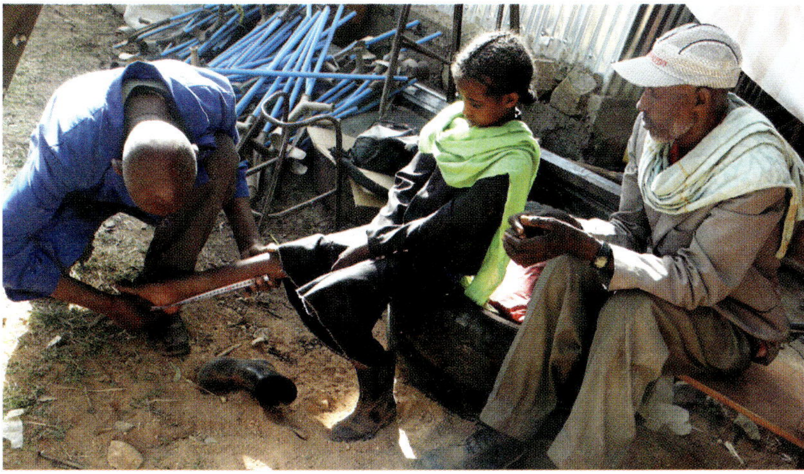

Outreach teams visit remote communities all over Ethiopia. In Jimagenet, 360km west of Addis Ababa, they are seen measuring, making, and fitting substitute or new appliances. The rural area is beautiful, but facilities are few. The bus back holds a mobile workshop

They don't work alone. In Jimagenet, for example, CSE's partner agency is the local branch of World Vision, in whose field the bus is parked, and which undertakes to transport those referred to Addis or elsewhere. The woreda's social worker is responsible for preparing the day's list. His colleagues check people in while he serves as an interpreter during diagnosis, which takes place behind an improvised sheet curtain in an open-sided barn. This is deepest Oromia, and many don't speak Ethiopia's lingua franca, Amharic.

Translation is the least of the challenges for Nurlign Mengste, the physiotherapist on the Jimagenet trip. Unlike his counterparts in the West, Nurlign is on the front line. His diagnosis could make the difference between life and death. For example, he sees a boy with spina bifida, carried there by his brother. Referral is urgent, and part of the problem is that the boy has been hidden away at home without treatment.

A 65-year-old man staggers up on improvised long sticks. He needs crutches which provide support under the armpits. CSE don't have anything which can be adapted on the spot. The physio asks for measurements which can be taken to Menagesha, the crutches made there, and delivered back to Jimagenet by World Vision when they're next doing the round trip.

A third patient is a 17-year-old post-polio girl who is prescribed an operation at the Balacha Hospital in Addis, followed by rehabilitation at Menagesha. For Nurlign and his team this is a standard referral. For the girl it's the chance to start a new life.

The same is true for an 8-year-old boy whose left leg has been amputated just below the knee. He says he fell out of a tree. Amputation followed medical treatment which had led to gangrene, unfortunately quite a common occurrence. He will be fitted with a prosthetic leg at Menagesha, but before that he'll need treatment on his knee joint to make it more supple.

Meantime the mobile workshop at the rear of the bus is in full blast. Some patients have been before (the team visits the area every six months). Their supportive boots have worn out through everyday use. Working from Nurlign's instructions, the technicians adapt the boots with new insteps and weld them to the leg braces.

The only proviso here is that clients leave their old boots behind. One teenager, who has a polypropylene leg support fitted with the boot but complains it is too tight, argues the toss. He wants to keep his old boots, which aren't badly worn. After a bit of debate he's allowed to go away with both.

The open-air waiting area, with improvised benches and plastic cans to sit on, fills up. Children brought by mothers or grandparents quietly pass the time at one end; at the other, those with new boots or devices gingerly try them out before taking off home.

On the second day at Jimagenet four people were waiting who couldn't make it the previous day. They simply had not been able to get transport from their homes 30km distant. They were seen first, without complaint from the others. CSE policy is never to turn anybody away, but with the kind of travel schedule outlined above there's inevitably a limit to what the team of four are able to do.

One reason the mobile units are so efficient is that they've been practising the routine for many years. It was in the mid-1980s that Cheshire began to receive requests, typically from Catholic institutions running clinics outside the Addis radar in places like Attat.

Staff of the time used whatever transport was available, and would make the drive there and back in a day if they could. This programme was first supported by Terre des Hommes Netherlands and Fr Jac Ermers. From the numbers of patients who found their way to Menagesha it was evident that a huge untreated demand existed beyond urban centres in the countryside.

During the 1990s, mobile outreach spread to cover the whole country; the strain was relieved a little when government authorities in Tigray and Amhara provinces announced they were able to cope themselves. But, says Fasıl Ayele, CSE's programme manager, cases from these regions have started to crop up again because the authorities there just don't have the same rehabilitation capabilities.

Fasil points out that the principal cause of disability is poverty. Many of the cases seen in Jimagenet could have been prevented, either by vaccination or by prompt, effective medical treatment for the primary complaint.

With the opening of the Hawassa branch in 2005 and its fully-equipped workshop (see pages 67-71) some outreach teams at least start significantly south of the capital, making driving to the southern regions less arduous. Others use the eastern centre at Dire Dawa as their base.

Follow-up visits every six months are the rule – and important because children quickly outgrow their appliances. With fuel prices proportionately

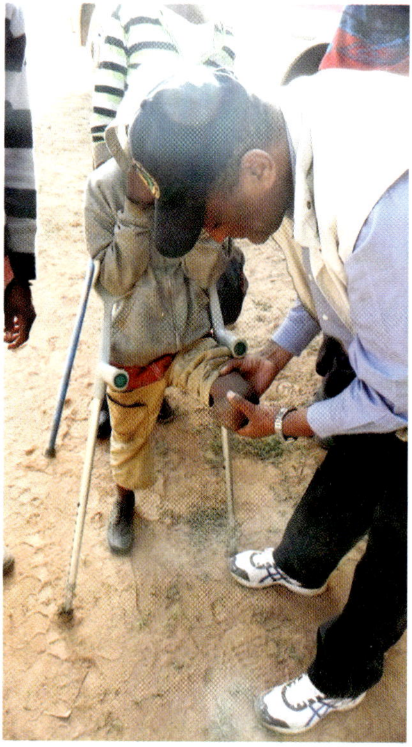

Fasil Ayele, CSE's programme manager, examines a boy's leg amputated below the knee. Treatment involves the boy coming to Menagesha

higher in Ethiopia than the West because of the Birr's plunging exchange rate, travel has become a major cost column. An extra problem lay in the government's ruling that fuel costs should be apportioned as an administrative rather than a programme expense in NGO budgets.

CSE, which works with central, regional and local governments on its outreach programmes, made strong submissions in this area – leaving them in no doubt that services would have to be curtailed. In Spring 2012 the authorities agreed to fuel being included in CSE's programme budget.

There's another issue: CSE's two buses, which ply the rural roads and have many hundreds of thousands of kilometres between them, are old. They let in the dust, a major hindrance in the dry season. And they are expensive to maintain, even though the organisation has its own mechanics (which it will send out to distant breakdowns, to avoid paying exorbitant garage charges).

Given the nature of mobile outreach, CSE could claim to be the only local NGO operating on a national scale. It's an extraordinary achievement, although it also shows up the treatment gap in Ethiopian society and is not trumpeted for that reason.

Like so much else in the organisation it goes quietly on month-in, month-out. Those who believe that Ethiopians are victims of a dependency culture bred by over-eager donors might care to look at such operations and think again.

"One of the elders who has a child affected by polio was very happy to see him walking"

A routine report from March 21 1995, when Cheshire's mobile outreach service had already been in operation almost ten years, offers a graphic picture of the challenges faced in one small part of a big country.

The report is of a visit to the remote area of North Omo, some 500km south of Addis Ababa, around the town of Arba Minch. It was compiled by an experienced social worker, Tesfay Abraha, who was working with a physiotherapist, Kifle Assefa, and two technicians, Addis Bitew and Mengistu Assefa, at the behest of the local Catholic mission.

"The team worked in Mirab on 27-2-95 and assessed 55 cases. Five cases are for admission. There was not good coordination in Mirab Abayia. The generator which was brought from another site was broken. Another generator was brought from Arba Minch and it was not good either. The fixing of the generator took time. At last, the workshop started its work which forced it to stay late up to 7.30pm (these days, mobile buses are equipped with their own generators).

"The next day we worked in Arba Minich. The children were from Arba Minch town, the surrounding peasant associations, Gedello, Jinka and Demeka. In Arba Minch there were 131 patients. Eight cases were for admission to Cheshire Home and Terre des Hommes.

"In Arba Minch there were three known elders from the nomadic areas of Jinka and Demeka. These elders were invited by the Catholic mission to see the work of Cheshire Home and to communicate to their community what they had seen. The team explained to the elders and parents who had come to the centre about the work of Cheshire Home, polio virus, and the importance of vaccination.

"The elders stayed with us for two days observing the work and they were pleased and happy. One of the elders has a child affected with polio

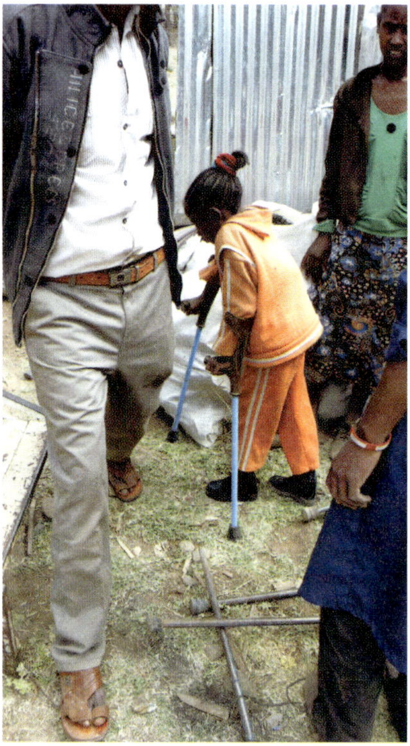

A young girl heads for home after being fitted with new walking aids at Jimagenet

and he was very happy to see his child walking well with the help of appliances. The elders promised to inform and to teach to their community the importance of vaccination and to send their children for treatment.

"They have cleared the misconception that if a child is sent to Addis Ababa he will lose his extremities. The Catholic mission was very pleased to see these elders who are influential groups to the community to be convinced to communicate what they have observed to the nomadic areas.

"Patients from Jinka and Demeka were well followed up. In Arba Minch area the follow up was not satisfactory and many patients were discharged from the programme.

"A new orthopaedic technician is employed in Arba Minch but while we were very busy and late in Mirab he didn't intend to help the workshop and didn't make and fit a single brace. In Arba Minch also he didn't do anything and we felt that the boy either is not interested or he has no ability. One handicapped (person) was very helpful in Arba Minch in making braces. After we finished in Arba Minch it was Ramadan Day and there was no work.....

"The work in Chencha was good. The follow up was also nice. The social section of Chencha has given a certificate of appreciation, Dorze's national dress and spear to Cheshire Home and Terre des Hommes.

"In Chencha there were 115 cases and 11 are for admission to Cheshire Home and TDH. In Sawlla also there were 65 cases and there are three for admission to Cheshire Home and TDH.

"In both places the follow-up is good and they have invited us also for next time."

Hawassa, CSE's multi-purpose centre and gateway to Southern Ethiopia

Entrance to CSE Hawassa

Cheshire Services Ethiopia began community-based rehabilitation initiatives seriously in the early 1990s. Children were coming for operations from further and further afield. When they returned to their communities after initial rehab at Menagesha they didn't, of course, stop growing. Appliances needed checking and recalibrating, general health monitoring, and home conditions were increasingly seen as a key to progress, or lack of it.

Ethiopia is a far-flung largely rural society composed of many ethnic groups. Once off the trunk roads, communications are slow at best. As the Cheshire outreach teams developed in the 1990s they found that they were spending a lot of time, money and energy simply getting to places. A plan was forged for regional bases to serve as centres of rehabilitation and community development, as well as for outreach services.

The Hawassa centre, opened in May 2005 and funded principally by Athiopien-Komitee Munchen ev and Sternstunden ev, two Munich-based charities, is CSE's most important presence outside Addis Ababa. Others at Dire Dawa and Harar in the east of the country have their own specialities.

Hawassa, some 270km south of Addis, is both the capital of and the gateway to Ethiopia's Southern Nations, Nationalities and Peoples' Region, with a population of at least 17 million, which extends south and west to borders with Kenya and South Sudan. SNNPR is one of nine federal states created in 1994 by the present government

The centre, on land at the outskirts of town provided by the Hawassa city authority, was purpose-built for use as a rehabilitation centre. It has workshops where orthopaedic appliances are made and adapted, a gymnasium, an IT-training studio and administrative offices.

In line with CSE's devolution philosophy, the centre controls its own budget, raises funds locally (notably by organising its own annual sponsored walk), and negotiates individual contracts with donors and/or government authorities.

Meseret Kidane, its director, a former print and broadcast media journalist with the Ethiopian News Agency, is a determined advocate of partnership as the way forward for relatively small NGO operations like his.

Partnership can involve international players like World Vision or Light for the World, central and local government and a mix-and-match combination of NGOs (70+ in Hawassa, 250 in the region).

Issues are similar to many in Addis Ababa, but approaches differ on a region-to-region basis. Meseret stresses CSE Hawassa's eagerness to involve local urban communities as well as serving, via its outreach bus, the enormous rural hinterland.

On the day I visited the centre was being evaluated by a group of government representatives whilst a team of community-based rehabilitation workers discussed their upcoming programmes. Young people from families with disability practised IT skills on (offline) computers, a physiotherapist was giving a small boy with knock knees his initial exercises, and prosthetic appliances were under production in the workshops.

CSE Hawassa is a member of the Association of Education and Training Services for Disabilities, South Ethiopia Hawassa. The centre is licensed by government agencies to train cooperative self-help groups, loaning them small sums to start businesses (which they repay at 5-7% annual interest). Each group is advanced 200 sq m of land on which to operate.

As CSE moves into an era where new cases of polio are increasingly rare, service demand is coming from disabled people of all categories, including those with sight and hearing issues. Resources are the main hurdle.

Education is also vital. An August 2011 report on community-based rehabilitation for Light for the World pointed up ignorance and

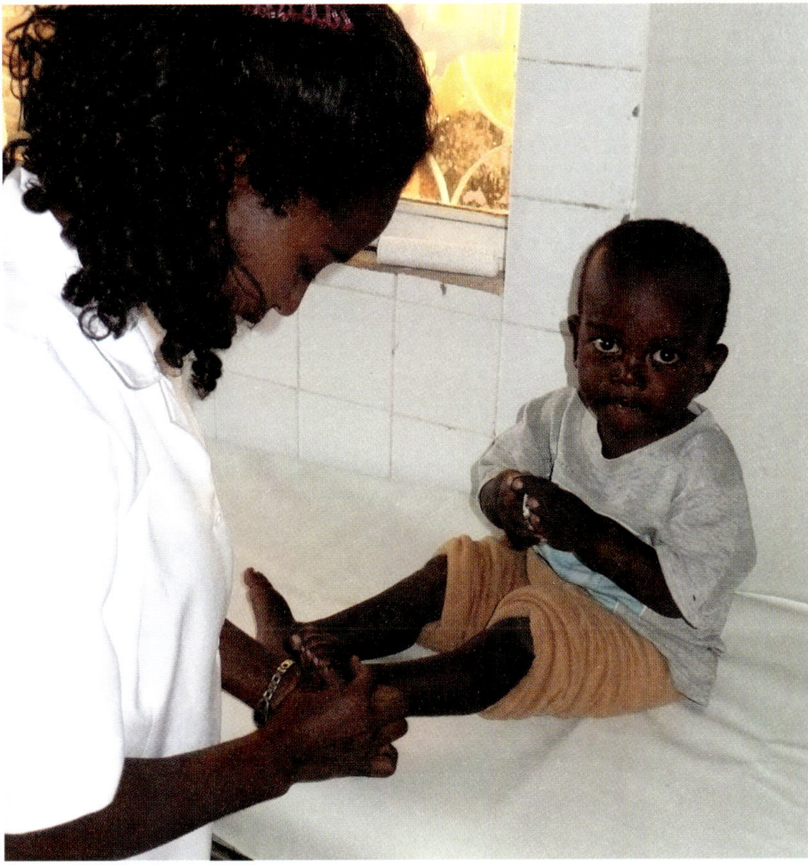

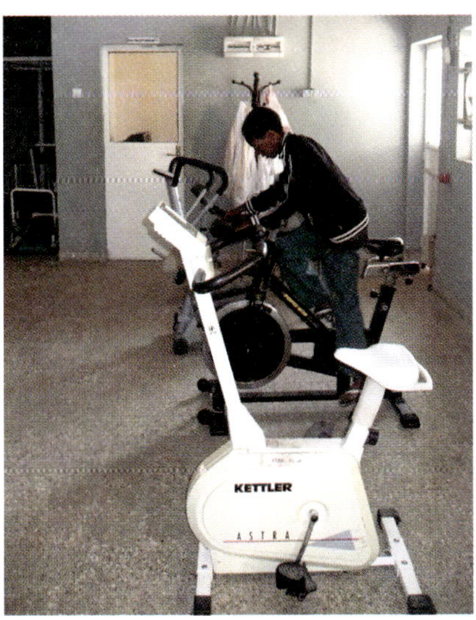

A CSE physiotherapist undertakes the initial inspection of a young boy with knock knees. Left: exercising in the well-equipped gym, open to use by nearby communities

superstition as compounding disability by stigma. "Before CSE came to Hawassa," the report states, "disabled children were assumed to be a sign of anger and punishment from God towards their parents... The family used to keep disabled children in a dark corner for the majority of their lifetimes, and some developed contractures of their legs."

However, since CSE's intervention in Hawassa "most children with cross-disabilities, mainly physically disabled, have been visited in their own localities to regularly assess and upgrade appliance fitting."

Additionally, "CSE-Hawassa assigned five community-based rehabilitation workers so that parents were easily involved in the process to enable children gain physical, emotional and psycho-social support in their own communities."

As the report points out, such activities comply with national development strategies towards poverty reduction, gender equality and the rights of people with disabilities. In effect, CSE-Hawassa is the agency delivering such objectives at grassroots level.

Although Hawassa guards its autonomy, Meseret looks to his colleagues in the capital with confidence. "I'm proud of the management team in Addis," he says, "they are a role model for NGOs."

Dire Dawa also has a community-based approach. Built on 12,000 sq m of land supplied by the city administration, the centre makes orthotic and prosthetic devices and runs coordinated rehabilitation activities across the city for children with cross disabilities. Given the centre's closeness to Somalia and other war-torn areas its outpatient care unit deals with relatively high numbers of amputees, and a small residential unit has been created to house patients while they wait for legs to be made and fitted.

In Harar, home-based rehabilitation and livelihood support schemes are supplemented by a pioneering kindergarten where disabled and non-disabled children are taught together in a practical demonstration that "inclusion" is not just a fine word.

CSE social workers discuss upcoming projects in and around Hawassa. Not just disabled people, but also their family members, benefit from computer training at CSE Hawassa

'I never lost sight of the Group Captain's vision'

In the December 2003 edition of the newsletter, *Walk On*, CSE's executive director, Gebremedhin Bekele, wrote an account of his 30 years with Cheshire. That tally now amounts to nearly 40 years. Gebremedhin rarely talks about himself in such a personal way. His experience with the organisation is unparalleled. In the interests of historical record his contribution to *Walk On* is reprinted here

"I had never dreamed of working with the disabled until a lecturer at the Haile Selassie 1 University (now Addis Ababa University) who happened to be a board member of the Cheshire Home suggested I should apply to be a social worker, which I did in November 1972. Four of us were interviewed and the board accepted me with reservations, as I was very young.

I was shocked to see disabled children when I visited the centre and the Princess Tsehai Hospital. I was no different from my folks with regard to causes of disability. I kept asking myself why God wanted the children to suffer when he could save or heal them, or let them die.

The Home was an orphanage of about 90 children and young adults, some of whom were boarders at Addis Ababa, Akaki and Kuyera Adventist Schools. My main job was to place the "orphans" and make the centre a rehabilitation place for physically handicapped children, mainly those affected with post-polio paralysis.

This was not an easy job but things went as I had planned and within six months 50 of the orphans were placed. I started a guarantor system whereby a parent or relative of a child to be admitted was requested to give a guarantor with a proper address. 'Parking' of disabled children was stopped with this system, which still works to benefit the Home today.

In 1973 an international conference of the Cheshire Central Regional Council was held at Addis Ababa. Group Captain Leonard Cheshire was

not happy with the way we were running the Cheshire Home. He said it should be a permanent refuge and that the disabled should stay as long as they wished. It was a blow for us but we did not succumb to his idea as we strongly believed that Europe and Africa had different needs.

Later in life Group Captain Cheshire admitted he had been wrong, and understood and appreciated the stand we took. He left it to the discretion of each region or country to decide which way to go in dealing with disability issues in their respective communities. Our centre has continued to be a short-stay physical rehabilitation programme for post-polio affected children.

The Communist revolution restricted the activities of NGOs in the country. Most of them were nationalised, but we escaped. We were open in our dealings and were on such good terms with the government that they employed a social worker to support our work. We were also privileged to organise fundraising and got the support of the government in bringing in foreign professionals, which was not normally possible in that restrictive regime.

Over the years I have learned the importance of transparency, and the importance of speaking one's mind. We have always fought any sign of embezzlement or misuse of funds in the organisation. We felt accountable to the public; as a result the public and government have confidence in the Home and have supported us in our endeavours.

Responding to the challenge of rehabilitation is considerably more difficult. To sort out some of the challenges we have moved from an institutional approach to an outreach type of service that developed into the more appropriate, effective, feasible and economically-viable approach of a community-based rehabilitation programme. I have witnessed the growth of the organisation as a major actor in designing and implementing a programme to cover most parts of the country serving persons with disabilities.

I am also happy to see the Home attain the highest standards in the rehabilitation of the physically disabled. For the last 30 years I have never lost sight of the vision of the man who founded the organisation. This has often meant sacrificing my own rights for the benefit of the organisation, which has given me moral and spiritual satisfaction. ”

Reinvention saves the day for Addis Ababa's top moneyspinner

Lilla Heaslip looks at how Cheshire's celebrated 21km walk has adapted to changing circumstances

As the pioneer of the fundraising-walk idea in Ethiopia, Cheshire has always been at the forefront. For many years the Cheshire walk was the only walk in town, but recently everyone has taken up the idea so it is important that the Cheshire walk is always different from the others.

In the difficult days of the Derg regime, the Cheshire walk attracted hundreds of young people and was something to look forward to each year (see pages 30-31). Luxuries for the man in the street were non-existent and one of the highlights of the walk was the bottle tombola run by the British community; wines and spirits were donated by the different embassies, whisky being especially popular; people did not mind how long they queued to have a turn. It was a real money-spinner.

The British and Canadian embassies ran the cake stall, which was another winner as sugar was rationed and in very short supply. Bands of street kids used to come along on spec; on one particular occasion, when chocolate cake or brownies suddenly appeared, the 'Artful Dodger' of the band (aged about 13) pulled a wad of notes out of his pocket and peeled them off to buy the brownies for his gang, having resisted for a long time in the hope of getting a discount!

Sir Derek Day, the British Ambassador of the time, also walked. As he recalls, his bodyguard insisted on accompanying him but preferred to follow behind at a discreet distance in an embassy Land Rover, much to others' amusement.

It is amazing how many current high-level officials in both government and business circles remember the days when they 'walked for Cheshire', and this has sometimes been instrumental in smoothing the paths of bureaucracy. However, times change, and by 1998 the walk was no longer bringing in the funds needed to support projects.

After much deliberation and a certain amount of angst, it was decided to change the profile, focussing on attracting individuals who would raise Birr 1000 per person (at that time approximately £100). The new format increased revenues significantly.

In recent years participation has changed from being a mixture of Ethiopians and expatriates to being predominantly Ethiopian, with increasing involvement of leading business organisations. This serves to create awareness among the walkers, their families and colleagues.

Lunch is generously provided by the Addis Hilton each year, and a competitive spirit has developed - with contests between the various organisations after lunch, which the children find highly entertaining; there is also music and the children too join in the dancing.

The route, constantly under review, has become a cross-country hike in the beautiful area around Menagesha. When this was introduced about eight years ago there was some consternation as going cross-country was an alien concept, but it rapidly became popular. This makes the Addis Ababa walk unique.

While the results are very positive, the downside is that fewer young people take part so other ways have to be found to create awareness about disability and promote inclusive activities. To this end, an integrated children's fun run was launched in 2006. Disabled and non-disabled children participated according to their capabilities; blind youngsters ran with 'buddies' from the guides or scouts movement; there was something for everyone.

Some 29 schools took part, the age range being 7-14. It was a popular event but sadly was discontinued after four years. Now, integrated events with visiting schools are becoming increasingly popular at Menagesha and indeed at all the Cheshire centres. Hawassa, Harar and Dire Dawa also stage their own annual fund-raising walks.

Although the walk will always be the major local source of revenue, there have been many other successful events over the years. In the early days, the proceeds of gymkhanas were donated to Cheshire while the Round Table held an annual ball after the walk.

Sabat Ferenghi, a popular jazz band in the 1990s, gave charity concerts for Cheshire as did Sheba Consort – a classical chamber orchestra composed of British, Japanese, Russian, German and Ethiopian musicians who were staunch supporters for many years. They also played for the children and bought them instruments to encourage music-making.

Then there were the Happy Angels - Japanese ladies who had played together in their youth and met up again in their retirement; they came twice to Addis and entertained the children before handing over money that they had raised giving concerts in Japan.

In the current economic climate fundraising becomes ever more challenging, especially given Ethiopia's rampant inflation. That is particularly worrying as the outreach programme (see pages 60-64) relies heavily on money raised locally to support the crucial follow-up care it provides to more than 5,000 children and young people throughout the country each year.

The climax of the annual walk at Menagesha is an afternoon of music, dancing and friendly competition between corporate sponsors. Participants set out in the cool of the morning. Any stragglers are invited to do the last kilometres on horseback. The 2011 walk, seen here raised Birr 574,080 ($32,360) for CSE

The smiling face of a serial fundraiser

Sir Alec Reed CBE is the ubiquitous face of Ethiopiaid, the British charity he founded in 1990 to fundraise for Ethiopia

Well into his seventies, Sir Alec could be enjoying luxury retirement amid a loving family, happy in the knowledge that he created a successful and pertinent international business, Reed Specialist Recruitment.

Family, yes, but Sir Alec's hardly the sort of person you find much at the golf club. There are too many causes for the Reed Foundation, his charitable arm, to champion. Not just Ethiopiaid but the Big Give, which showcases the work of 9,000 charities worldwide. Sir Alec is a serial fundraiser.

At his Knightsbridge office he prowls around young teams bashing the phone lines. He's very upfront about the formula. "We send out volumes of cold junk mail." But with the current recession people are giving less, and Sir Alec also worries about donor fatigue over Ethiopia's apparently endless challenges.

Among other Ethiopian causes supported are the Fistula Hospital, Missionaries of Charity – The House of Angels, Forum for Street Children Ethiopia, Hope and Hope University College, and Facing Africa whose operational base in Ethiopia is Menagesha (see pages 82-85).

A chartered management accountant who began life as an office boy, Sir Alec assesses the projects he supports in a very direct way – by giving marks out of ten. CSE normally expects to make at least nine, but there is no guarantee. His teams visit Addis on a regular basis, and he himself pops up every year or so to get a feel for how things are going.

He was in Addis in October 2010 to open Reed House, the head office of CSE which doubles as a rehabilitation centre for young outpatients from the Addis area, and again in February 2012 when he and his wife made an unheralded visit.

It's no secret that Ethiopiaid is CSE's main source of funding, a fact that keeps Gebremedhin and staff on their toes. It helps that Sir Alec holds Lilla Heaslip, CSE's former chair and present head of fundraising, in very high regard. "Lilla has been a fantastic asset to Cheshire," he comments.

He's not the sort of person to mince words. He wonders aloud whether Ethiopia should be taking so much of the money he raises. "During the time I've known it the population has doubled and the currency value halved" he says wryly.

But then he's known for his quips. "I coined a phrase 'financial obesity is ugly: give handsomely'" he told a magazine interviewer. "Companies represent a host of shareholders. I think giving ought to be a personal thing really – you should give your own money away, not somebody else's."

Sir Alec's trick lies in persuading you to give your personal money to a cause of his personal choice. And CSE is a major beneficiary.

Sir Alec Reed at the October 2010 opening of Reed House

Half habesha, half ferengi, wholly the creative networker

"Leonard Cheshire was a childhood hero of mine." Lilla Heaslip, CSE's former chairman and chief fundraiser, is no different from others of her generation growing up in post-war Britain. Cheshire VC was a hero full stop. He remains one.

But then Lilla – the name by which she's known to all – met Cheshire in Jakarta, 1987, where the great man celebrated his 73rd birthday. It was her first involvement, too, with the Cheshire movement.

"He was an amazing individual. He didn't look over his shoulder. He was totally involved in whatever he undertook. He was also a very religious person, in the best sense."

Like Leonard Cheshire before her, Lilla is a practising Catholic, though unlike him she was born one – to an Irish doctor's family in Sale, Cheshire (yes, another connection). Just to be more different, she married an Irish Protestant from Cork, and it was with her husband James that she came to Ethiopia in 1991.

"People told me they knew I was trouble, but they didn't suspect I'd start a war." She is referring, of course, to the revolution concurrent with her arrival which brought the present regime to power and saw an end to the hated Derg.

It was a good time to start life in Addis, a time which saw CSE reaching out to new donors and pioneering ventures like the outreach service which today extends to much of Ethiopia.

Lilla's first personal taste of disability was when she broke a leg skiing. "Being on crutches taught me a lot." In recent years her eyesight has deteriorated – not that this prevents her from running a day job examining English for the British Council in Addis Ababa, organising sponsored walks and other events, spreading the word and commuting to her Sussex home during seasonal breaks.

As CSE's chair from 1996-2004 Lilla formed a highly-productive

working relationship with Gebremedhin Bekele, CSE's executive director. She says, however, that she never felt at ease in the official role. "I became a very unlikely chairperson. It was not quite right for a ferengi. I was and am much happier as a fundraiser. My role is creative networking." She received an MBE in 2002 for services to Cheshire.

An excellent example of her negotiating skills can be seen in the outreach buses which travel many thousands of km each year deep into the rural hinterland with specialist technical and medical teams (see pages 60-64). These buses were jointly funded by a number of donors who she brought on board. She was also instrumental in securing Japanese Embassy funding for the Menagesha recovery centre.

James Heaslip died in August 2010. The tribute to him, and by inference to Lilla, posted on the notice-board at CSE's Hawassa centre, reads: "the late Mr Heaslip has been a staunch supporter of Cheshire Services Ethiopia and has been behind the whole contribution and efforts of his family, particularly Mrs Lilla Heaslip."

She claims to be retiring in December 2012, but don't bank on Lilla staying put in East Sussex. "I'm half Ethiopian. Ethiopia and Cheshire are in my blood. I will always be involved, one way or another".

Menagesha offers solace and security to patients receiving new faces

Some 15 years ago Chris Lawrence, a successful holiday travel operator based in South West England, sold his business. He and his wife Terry had decided to devote the remainder of their lives to a humanitarian cause. While cautiously looking around, he happened across a German documentary film on noma, a bacterial infection prevalent in many parts of Sub-Saharan Africa, which devastates the faces of the children it attacks, if it doesn't kill them – 90% die within three or four weeks.

Following visits to Hanover, where the annual gathering of the noma community is held, Lawrence started to sound out interest in British surgical circles. Restorative surgery for patients with noma involves complex reconstructive work on faces often horribly disfigured. It's highly specialised work, not just for surgeons but for the whole medical team.

After looking around African countries, Lawrence decided on Ethiopia as first-choice operational base for Facing Africa, the charity he and Terry had created. There was a role model in Dutch teams which had made several visits to Ethiopia, and which Facing Africa started to part-fund. In 2007 the first British surgical team was finally assembled and flown in.

As a concept, bringing British surgeons on "missions" of a few weeks to Ethiopia is hardly new. The Fistula Hospital, established by Drs Reginald and Kathryn Hamlin just outside Addis Ababa to address injuries caused to women by poor childbirth methods, regularly welcomes UK specialists – who volunteer skills and time. Lawrence couldn't offer a well-run hospital to attract potential medics, and there was the additional challenge of getting together the rest of the team plus essential equipment. He overcame considerable reluctance to the proposition.

Lawrence led the first mission, as he still does lead each one. But, he says, the team found patients were "put in hostels you wouldn't lodge a dog in". The government hospital used for operations was also unsatisfactory, and successful post-operative nursing care was prejudiced by less than

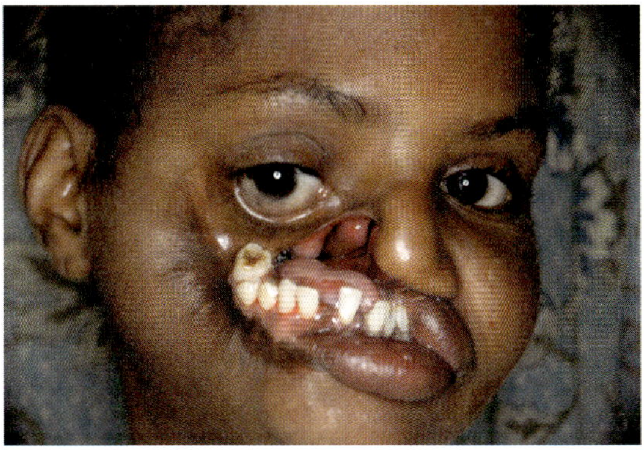

Noma is a devastating disease. These illustrations show just two of the many helped to date by Facing Africa. Rachid, left, had noma as a one-year-old. He has benefited from three operations so far by surgical teams from Great Ormond Street Hospital, London. Fatiha, below, is from Harar. She was 16 at the time of her first operation

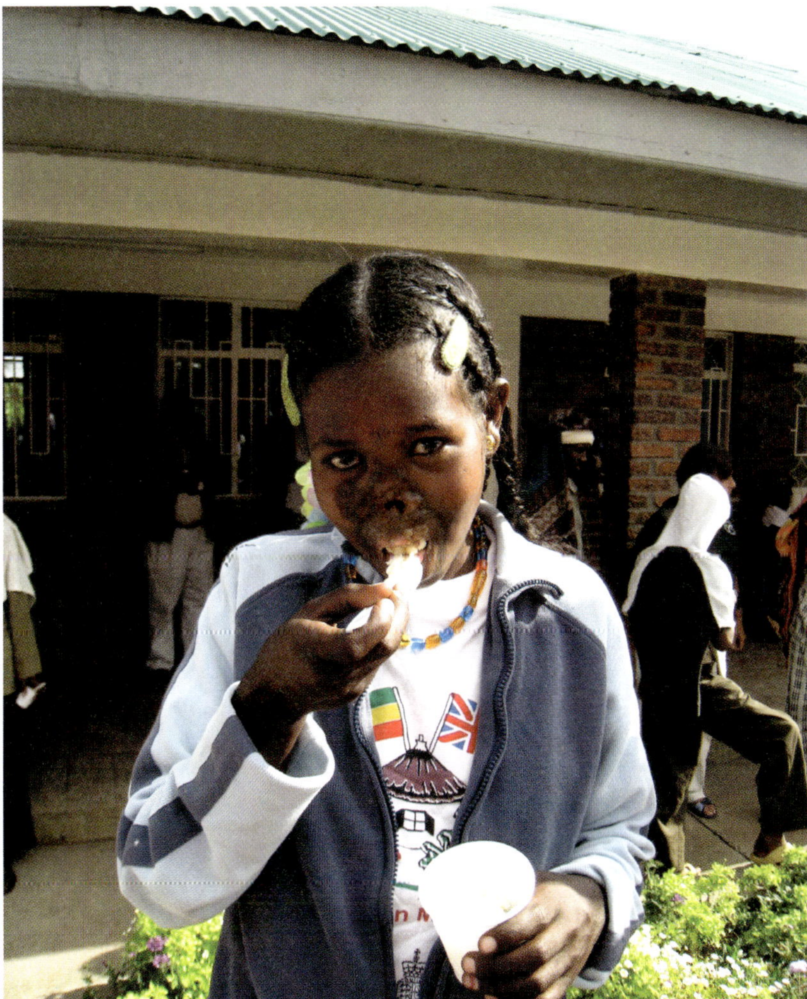

sanitary hostel conditions. "It's sometimes better not to operate at all than to leave a skin-graft open to infection" he comments.

In Addis, however, Lawrence met Gebremedhin Bekele, Cheshire Services Ethiopia's executive director. Through discussion they came to the conclusion that Menagesha was the ideal place for a purpose-built centre where noma patients would come for two weeks of preparation before operations and three/four weeks of post-operative care afterwards. The principle is similar to CSE's year-on-year involvement with polio cases.

Apart from securing agreement with CSE, Lawrence negotiated to have operations performed at the Korean Hospital which, in his words, is "by African standards exceptionally good." CSE's main sponsor, Ethiopiaid, is also a partner of Facing Africa at Menagesha.

The centre, formally opened in February 2011, has two dormitories with bed-space for 10 girls and 10 boys, plus a recreation room and other facilities. Building contracts, handled by CSE, ran over budget at a time of heavy cost inflation but Lawrence has no regrets about the choice of Menagesha.

The new building is tucked away discretely from CSE's admin centre into the surrounding woodland, with a wide expanse of lawn and shrubs. At the same time there's the knowledge that Cheshire people are nearby, and that the estate is both safe and peaceful.

In fact, according to Daniel Beyissa, the project officer who manages Menagesha, noma patients take part in the relaxed routines of life at the rehabilitation centre, making friends amongst the other children. Because their stay at Menagesha is shorter than the others, the noma children probably don't cement such deep friendships, but it's here that they slowly realise they will be fine to return to their towns and villages with new faces.

A second dormitory block, already under construction at Menagesha, will raise the potential number of patients treated each mission to 40. This phase also includes a reorganisation of wound dressing and laundry facilities and of essential amenities.

Getting the practicalities right is only half the problem. Chris Lawrence is himself no slouch at fund-raising. He would like Facing Africa to make more than two eight-week missions to Addis. "Money is not the issue," he says. "It's the Ethiopian customs-clearance process which is our worst nightmare." Facing Africa ships in up to 40 cases of drugs and equipment with each mission, which may take hours and even days to clear even though Lawrence travels ahead to pave the way each time, and he has two local employees.

Facing Africa acquired official Ethiopian Government charity status in March 2012 and it is hoped that this will ease the importation of essential equipment, drugs, consumables and disposables for each mission.

Apart from carrying out 90-100 facial reconstructions each year, Facing Africa's other aim is to teach Ethiopian surgeons, anaesthetists and nurses improved and modern skills both in the operating room and in post-op wound care. In July 2012 the charity funded two Ethiopian plastic surgeons to attend micro-surgical courses in the UK, which should make them the first Ethiopians to perform micro-surgery in their own country.

Dr Abiye Hailu Gebread, an Ethiopian plastic surgeon from the Zewditu Memorial Hospital who worked with the team from the UK during the two missions in 2011, is himself critical of Ethiopia's current inability to tackle the complexities of conditions like noma.

Facing Africa's partnership with CSE is not without tensions – perhaps understandable when a youngish, UK-based organisation joins forces with a mature Ethiopian operation. There have been misunderstandings and cultural differences on both sides. Chris Lawrence is a very direct person, an attribute when responding to the challenge of noma. He has found Gebremedhin and team just as forceful in their own way.

Lawrence is an outspoken advocate of his cause, seizing every opportunity to promote it, a PR natural. But when UK newspapers won't print the photographs he sends them because they believe them to be too shocking for readers it seems that cultural changes need to take place just as much in Europe as in Africa.

Cheshire's chairman, looking beyond polio, represents historic Rotary links

As a leading member of the business community, CSE's current chairman Nahu-Senaye Araya is only too aware of the organisation's high dependency on one prime source of income, the British charity Ethiopiaid. He also knows that polio, CSE's main activity area for much of its 50 years, is no longer a disease on priority lists for medical funding.

"We're a very well-run NGO," underlines the former CEO of Nyala Insurance. "Immediate finance is not a problem. But we are, of course, always concerned about sustainability. Polio may soon be eradicated and we are moving into new areas like helping those with club feet and noma. There remains a potential ten-year backlog of polio patients which we are also addressing.

"The regional authorities with whom we work understand the issues. We don't receive much cash from them but we do get a lot of support in terms of land, and in services in kind. We have extremely good relations with them."

Relations between central government and NGOs have a prickly history, but Cheshire has managed to remain independent, and on good terms with the authorities, by sticking closely to its mission.

"We are non-political in the true sense", says Nahu-Senaye. "We would not shout about human rights even if we were allowed to. We talk to families, but we don't campaign."

In the continual search for funding sources, the chairman is not particularly optimistic about Ethiopia's burgeoning business sector. "Businessmen claim that their margins have been squeezed. Most development is on the back of loans, and banks will repossess property if there is oversupply," he explains.

But there's nothing to stop local NGOs like CSE generating funds themselves. One Cheshire objective is to complete an office block on the same site as its Addis office, which should produce a steady rental income.

The theoretical aim for all local NGOs is to generate 90% of annual budget, at which point the Government treats them like a business rather than a charity. It's a target which remains tantalisingly distant.

Nahu-Senaye is also chairman of Ethiopia's National Rotary PolioPlus Committee, as well as being Rotary International's representative to the African Union and to UNECA.

Polio is one of the main causes championed worldwide by Rotary Club members, so it's not surprising that the Addis Ababa branch has been an active supporter during the 50 years of Cheshire's presence in Ethiopia.

The Rotarian – the movement's international magazine – featured Addis developments in its January 1965 issue. Among those pictured, Denise Tabernacle was to be seen as she "soothes a tot at the Cheshire Home for Retarded Children to which the Rotary Club of Addis has donated physiotherapy and other equipment." The article mentioned donations of "equipment to be used by needy cripples and mental defectives."

Such language would not be sanctioned today. But the Round Table and Rotary Club went on to sponsor Cheshire's highly successful 21km fundraising walk (its main source of funding during the Derg years) and to maintain their support in good times and bad.

Life stories

⁂

Over the years Cheshire has transformed the existence of thousands of Ethiopians who might otherwise have carried untreated disability throughout their lives. They have returned to their towns and villages often able to walk, work and care for themselves and families for the first time. Their stories are as varied as the cases themselves.

We asked four young people, each of whom has achieved extraordinary personal development in the time since they first came to Menagesha, to describe in detail how they responded to the realisation that they were disabled, to the treatment they received, and to the opportunities opening up for them. Their frank contributions explore the issues surrounding disability debates in modern Ethiopian society. They are also a testament to sheer perseverance.

LIFE STORY: ELLENI MOGES

"Cheshire was the only place where they saw a glimpse of hope for me walking"

My name is Elleni. I am 36 years old and currently live in the United States. I was born and raised in Ethiopia, coming to the US about 11 years ago. I contracted polio as a child. As a result I have paralysis in both legs and walk with the help of leg braces and crutches.

I was too young to remember my initial experience at Cheshire but, according to my family, after taking me to so many other places desperate to get me help, Cheshire was the only place they saw a glimpse of hope for me ever walking.

At the time, after a brief stay at Menagesha, I was fitted with braces and crutches and learned how to walk and went back home to my family in Tigray. Because I outgrew my braces, I had to go back to Cheshire for a second time. I remember staying for several years. I received corrective procedures for rehabilitation and was retrained in walking. All that time, I went to the nearby school.

I have fond childhood memories at Menagesha including lots of fun in the playground (swings were my favourite), playing with other kids, watching television, and going on picnics to the nearby forest at weekends.

Cheshire is also the place where I learned the basics of self-sufficiency such as making my own bed, folding my clothes, cleaning up after myself and even helping other kids. These chores were no fun for me at the time, especially because, back home, I was used to being taken care of by everyone as I am the youngest of ten children.

I also remember missing my family. When they came to visit, I would want to go home with them but they would convince me that I couldn't leave the school. I think I bought into that idea for a long time.

I left Cheshire in my pre-teen years and went back to live with my family. I remember realising how different life was outside Cheshire. While at high school, I decided I wanted to become an accountant. With that in mind, I went on to Addis Ababa University (AAU) where I received my bachelor's degree in accounting.

As much as they were fun, my AAU years also made me realise there is a lot to be done to make university accessible for people with disability. Although it is just a tip of the iceberg, I was fortunate enough to get collaboration from the head of the student council at the time to construct accessible toilets in the dormitory.

Before I moved to the US, I worked as an accountant for the then Ethiopian Telecommunications Corporation. I also served as a board member for Cheshire, which gave me a chance to get involved as an adult. After moving to the US I was fortunate enough to have the opportunity to become a certified public accountant. I work as a senior accountant in a financial services corporation.

As I congratulate Cheshire on its 50th anniversary, I can't help but think of how many peoples' lives including mine have been positively impacted by its work, for which I will be forever grateful.

"It's better to try and fail than not to try at all"

In Amharic Sisay means treasure. I was born in Debre Tabor in South Gondar in 1988. I was able to walk until I was two years old, then I got polio. I was taken to hospitals, churches and other places by my mother in the hope that that one day I would be able to walk again. However, I was unable to play with my friends, go to school, or walk.

My other relatives believed I had been cursed and tried to ignore me. Rather than helping me, they prayed for my death. My mother, however, ignored them because I was her son. She never gave up and continued searching for appropriate treatment.

My mother was not educated. She connected my disability to traditional thinking about "bad spirits". She did not know that polio was due to lack of vaccination.

As time went on, I started to ask myself what my problem was. I could talk, see, and play, just like any child. I used to play with other children and relatives but the only way I could move around was by crawling. When relatives came to our house they used to weep, and so did my Mum. I asked "Why do they cry whenever they come to our home?" I was unable to understand the reason for their unhappiness. My mother told them to stop crying and said she would handle everything.

I was so lonely and sad when my friends started school that my mother decided to carry me there on her back. She thought I would curse her if she kept me at home, while everyone else went to school. For some days she carried me but then other students said that they would take me. In grades one and two I was top of my class. My teachers were impressed, and told my mother that she should be proud of having such a clever son.

One day when I was sitting alone at home while Mum was at market, a fellow student came to tell me that I should go to the Bureau of Labour & Social Affairs (BoLSA) as there was a visiting medical team from Addis Ababa. Mum came back from market and I told her about the people who had come from Addis. As soon as I told her, she took me to BoLSA and I met the Cheshire outreach team in their mobile clinic. I was registered and assessed by Ato Kifle, the physiotherapist.

I had expected to be able to walk immediately after assessment, but we were told that I would need surgery. Two months later, my mother brought me to Addis and I was admitted to the Menagesha Rehabilitation Centre. No one in Debre Tabor ever imagined that I would be able to walk. After a year at Menagesha, surgery at the Black Lion Hospital and intensive physiotherapy at Cheshire, I was able to walk. I was no longer dependent on people. I could move about freely. Without the intervention of CSE, it would have been impossible for me to walk.

I went back to Debre Tabor and continued my education. I could now walk to school. I started to do well in class and was the top student out of all five classes in my year. Wo Hagere Belete, one of my teachers at primary school, was so happy with my results she offered to cover all my education costs. I was sorry I could not help my Mum at that time but I promised myself that one day I would be able to support her.

I was also active in extra-curricular activities. When I was in 11th grade at school, I was chairperson of the students union. I think my involvement in those activities helped to make me assertive and self confident.

One day, the administrator of my district had a serious argument with his wife. Some people went and begged him to make peace with her but he ignored them. I heard about this and went directly to the district administrator and discussed all the issues; finally, the problem was resolved. When people heard what I had done, they were impressed. This kind of activity has really helped me develop my self-confidence and inspire others.

I believe that anything is possible. It's better to try something and fail than not to try at all. My dream was to join Addis Ababa University, which I did in 2008. During my time as an undergraduate I was involved in many extra-curricular activities, holding positions of influence in student clubs and forums.

In the AAU Students Union, I promoted the rights of Students with Disabilities (SwDs), resulting in representation for blind and hearing-impaired students in the union. Generally, I have presented the concerns of students with disabilities to the university management. In recognition for my efforts in making a difference in the teaching-learning process in the university, I was awarded a scholarship to do my Masters by the former AAU president, Professor Enderias Eshete.

As a member of Young Voices, a global initiative for potential young leaders organised by Leonard Cheshire Disability, I represented Ethiopia at the LCD Global Alliance Meeting in Bangkok in March this year. It was an amazing experience meeting so many young people with disabilities from all over the world, which only served to fuel my determination to fight for our rights.

I believe I can make a difference with my engagement in the community. Following my Masters degree, I hope to study in other fields

LIFE STORY: AYCHESH MOLLA

"It is when we with disabilities raise our voices that others hear"

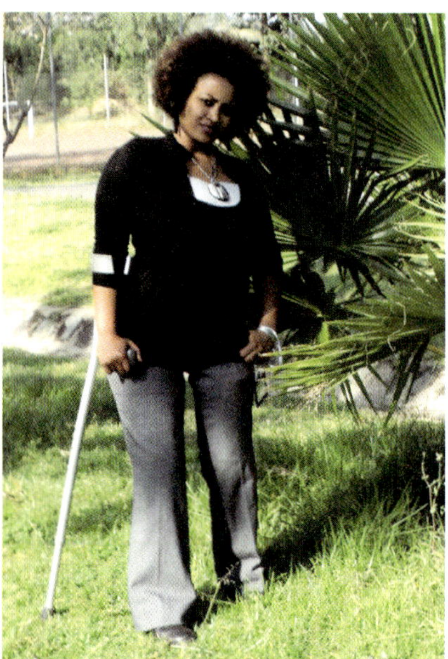

My Mum was sick after she gave birth to me. As every member of the family was running to save her life, my polio vaccination was forgotten. After all, my parents were ignorant about polio vaccination that time. When I was one year old, I suffered from fever, and my legs became weaker. Even when my parents took me to hospital, my case was not diagnosed: instead, I was given an injection to relieve my fever.

Looking for a cure, my mum took me to the traditional physiotherapist but there was no change. Finally, I was taken to the Black Lion Hospital in Addis Ababa where a nerve doctor discovered that my case was polio and referred her to Cheshire.

This is the saddest part. When my parents learnt that I could not walk normally like my other two sisters they and my relatives wished for me to die rather than see me crawling. My Mum used to cry day and night out of regret for the sinful deeds that, she thought, had caused her to have a disabled daughter.

The mindset of Ethiopian society is such that they think disability is caused by a curse from God, or by sinful deeds. People with disability are considered to be useless and a burden on the family. That is why my parents were so sad about my disability and even gave me the name Aychesh that means "Eager to see your future."

However, despite my parents' wrong perceptions about disability, they did not lock me up at home, as most parents do in Ethiopia. Instead, on the doctor's recommendation, my Mum took me to Cheshire Services Ethiopia when I was two years old. At Cheshire, I was fitted with braces and started walking for the first time with a walking frame, then with two crutches. When I was five I had intensive physiotherapy treatment at Menagesha which brought about a remarkable change. I started walking properly, with just one brace and one crutch.

It was after that that I started to be excluded and denied my rights. For instance, a neighbour forbade her daughter to play with me, telling her that my disability would transfer to her. The other children nearby heard about this and also refused to play with me. That broke my little heart. I realised that I was different from the rest and started to ask my parents why I could not walk just like the children in my village.

When I was six years old I was sent to a nearby kindergarten and then to an elementary school called Keste Demena. At both KG and elementary school I used to feel bad during break times, as I was not allowed to play with other children. Rather, I was obliged to sit alone and watch while my peers were shouting and enjoying themselves.

Seeing my loneliness at school, my father advised me to try to be an outstanding student and win friends that way. I focused on my studies and became just that, outstanding. As my father had predicted, the teachers were very pleased with me and started supporting me by every available means. Then my fellow students followed and became my friends.

I was happy, except that I could not use the toilets, which were without seats, and dirty. To avoid having to use the toilets at school, I was not eating and drinking properly.

I attended high school at Addis Ketema, which was not far from my village. My high school life was OK as I was still an outstanding student. At the end of the year, my parents were invited to attend the awards ceremony, at which I won first place most of the time.

My parents started feeling better about my disability and the whole family started being proud of me. Unlike the previous times, all the family members could see that I probably wouldn't be a burden on the family.

After completing high school successfully, I joined Addis Ababa University with good grades. At the university, I studied Sociology and Social Anthropology. However, my time at university was very challenging, mainly due to the inaccessibility of facilities - including the toilets, the stairs to the dorms, classes and library. Even if I managed the stairs with only a bit of support from my friends, the toilets' inaccessibility became more than I could bear.

As a result, I took the initiative to organise students with physical impairment in the university to discuss our challenges and state our issues to concerned officials. The group eventually got permission from the dean of students to form an Association of Students with Physical Disabilities. I was selected as the chairperson to lead the association.

Through our association we were able to fight for our rights to access all the facilities, the same as other students. Fortunately, thanks to Professor Enderias Eshete, President of Addis Ababa University, there was positive cooperation to help students with disabilities. For example, ramps to the Kennedy Library were constructed and handrails fixed to the stairs.

I realised then that it is when we, those with disabilities, raise our voices that others hear and understand our challenges. Instead of blaming others for things no being done, I decided to play my own part in bettering our life.

Right after graduation, I applied to CSE as a social worker and secured the placement. I was honoured to be working for Cheshire, as it was satisfying for me to contribute something towards its development. It was a source of inspiration for me to be giving psycho-social support to children with disabilities, children who are highly marginalised in different parts of Ethiopia.

Seeing the children change from crawling to walking and from depression and feeling useless to people with normal perceptions about their own value reminded me how Cheshire had changed my life for the better. I always think that if Cheshire had not been there to provide walking appliances for free, people like me would have never been gone to school and reached the stages where we are now.

After working for two years, Cheshire helped me go to United Kingdom to take part in a Leonard Cheshire Disability work experience programme for three months. During my placement time, I learned more about how to cope with the differing needs of disabled people as I was assigned to work on the development of a diversity toolkit for caregivers.

One objective of the toolkit was to direct caregivers on how to deliver services in a manner that satisfies the cultural and religious needs of people from all over the world. Moreover, it was a great opportunity for me to explore the latest rehabilitation methods as we were working in permanent residential homes for persons with severe disabilities.

After my return to Ethiopia, I shared what I learnt with Cheshire staff and tried to use the lessons myself. However, I was not satisfied with everything I was doing and saw I needed to pursue my education. The challenge lay in Menagesha being outside Addis. It was tough to study while working there.

So I changed my workplace to Addis Ababa and the Ethiopian Centre for Disability and Development (ECDD), securing a placement as a project coordinator for the *Guide to Accessible Addis Ababa.* The guide was published and a series of accessibility information seminars given to property developers, architects, engineers, urban planners and so on. In response to our efforts, some owners have made modifications to their buildings in a way that helps persons with disabilities.

Currently, I am working on another project, the *Guide to Accessible Ethiopia* promoting accessibility across the country as a continuation of the previous project. Moreover, I started studying a year ago for my Masters in social work in the extension programme at Addis Ababa University.

Behind these achievements, however, there were and still are many daily struggles to overcome exclusion from social activities and inaccessible premises. To attend evening classes, I face problems with Addis's inadequate public transport systems. Most mini-bus drivers are unwilling to let persons with disabilities get on board as they think that it will take too much time. As a result, I am obliged to use contract taxis, which are much more expensive than the public ones.

It makes me sad to think that hundreds of thousands of Ethiopian people with disabilities, who would have been able to contribute considerably to their country, still live in total exclusion and abandonment. Had they been given the correct opportunity, or if conditions were bettered for them, many would have emerged as great thinkers and hardworking members of our society.

LIFE STORY: BERHANU KIFLE

"Today I'm a competent person like my Mum said I would be"

My name is Berhanu Kifle. I was born in Addis Ababa in 1980. My father died when I was a year old. When I was three, I fell while I was playing with my friends and broke my leg badly. When this happened my family were shocked, especially my Mum.

The one thing that I will never forget until my death is what my Mum told me our neighbour said one day to her. He had said "Berhanu will never have a chance to learn to walk by himself, to challenge any problem, to do anything for himself". But my mother replied: "One day he will be a competent person".

It was a year and a half before I could walk at all and it was only when I was seven that my mother took me to Menagesha, where I was rehabilitated and fitted with a long-leg brace and orthopaedic shoes. I can say that my mother played a great role in my life; she made me learn and helped me to become what I am now. I would also like to thank CSE for helping me by providing the rehabilitation service and walking appliances from the very beginning.

Today I have a diploma in Computerised Accounting from Microlink Information Technology College and a BA with Distinction in Management Accounting from Admas University. I would like to go on to do further study, if I get the chance.

The amazing thing is that I have been working at CSE as an accountant since 2002, so you see I am going to celebrate ten years of working professionally with Cheshire and 50 years of CSE in action.

Today, like my Mum said I would be, I am a competent person because I can do everything I want. I have the confidence to do things with my peers and can play games such as football, volleyball and table tennis. I can walk long distances on any surface.

I sometimes advise disabled people not to feel disappointed but to persevere. I would like to thank God for everything: He made me forget my disability and He gave me what I needed to become an educated person. I truly believe that disability is not inability and I have proved it!

⁂

"We have been good for the Leonard Cheshire name"

50 years on, the organisation Cheshire inspired is more involved than ever in confronting disability issues within Ethiopian society

It sounds ridiculous to suggest that Leonard Cheshire was not a man of action. The most decorated British bomber pilot in history, whose skills and courage helped turn the tide of the Second World War, recast himself in the 1940s to build, piece by piece, a great humanitarian enterprise dedicated to other peoples' lives. Yet in a sense Cheshire was the still centre of the world he impacted so greatly.

His own lifespan happened to cover the most traumatic period in modern history. He was a leading participant in the aerial destruction of the Third Reich, combatants and non-combatants, including industrial targets in Occupied France and the 1944 attack on Munich. He was one of two British observers when the US Air Force dropped its second atomic bomb on Nagasaki in August 1945, changing war for ever. He commented in his 1961 book, *The Face of Victory*, how he felt it was "imperative to do something to see that it should never happen again."

He demonstrated during the early post-war years that a single human being, without much financial backing or any specific training, could make a huge difference to individuals in need. And yet the world seemed to happen around him.

Cheshire's deep humanity inspired others in unpredictable ways. He believed that any man, woman or child should be able to live their days free of prejudice, and particularly free of the prejudice surrounding disability. He made things happen, but he was essentially spiritual and the practicalities of daily life were not his strongest suit.

One extraordinary thing about the Cheshire home established in Addis Ababa and described in this short book has been its resilience. Addis did not have the typical expat community of the former British colonies to support the venture, but in fact Addis became the most successful of Cheshire's African ventures. Even in the dark days of the Derg – perhaps especially in the dark days of the Derg – the Home counted on support across the spectrum of Ethiopians and ferengis. It was almost always penniless, but it never lost hope. There was support to be found, one way or another.

This raises the question why CSE is today dependant on overseas funding for about 80 per cent of its work, compared with almost nothing 50 years ago. Ethiopian society – from federal, regional and local government through the business community, social organisations and individuals – contributed just Birr 6.58 million (or £244,000) for the three years ending April 2011. This for a service which – together with vaccination - has successfully dealt with Ethiopia's polio crisis, providing rehabilitation, aftercare and family support at no cost to the consumer.

Well, you could say, Ethiopia is one of the world's poorest countries, ranking 174 out of 187 on the World Bank human development index. It remains sadly dependant on donor aid. True, but look around at the money being displayed in the Addis Ababa Sheraton and Hilton hotels. The big spenders are from Addis's business community.

Look at the swathe of new building projects in the capital, whose architects have better job prospects at home than in London or New York. Look at the expansion of Ethiopian Airlines, and the development of Bole Airport as an international hub. Look at the local economy, growing an average ten per cent annually in recent years. There is new cash in Ethiopia, but it's unlikely to come Cheshire's way.

Work done by local NGOs like CSE is nowhere near the top of the government health agenda. The chances of obtaining significant direct funding, nationally or internationally, are slim. It's a fact of life which, no matter how good the PR and marketing, means that revenues only change by percentage points. And CSE is already Ethiopia's most successful NGO at raising funds locally.

So it's a question, as always, of how funding is spent. The charge levelled against NGOs as a category is that, no matter how good their work, they breed a dependency culture. One has to differentiate between international organisations and local NGOs. The former have a reputation for taking back almost as much as they give via salaries, holidays and perks to staff who'd be lucky to hold down similar jobs in the US or the UK; the latter have a reputation for inefficiency, corruption and – yes – accepting handouts while making little effort themselves.

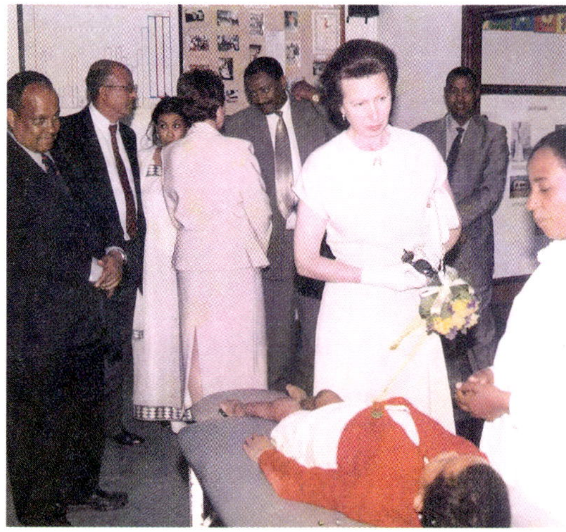

Zenebech Alegnta, one of ten children from a poor family, had polio at six months but after being operated on aged six and spending eight months in rehab at Menagesha she returned home. Zenebech eventually became a trained physiotherapist working for CSE, and is seen here explaining her job to Princess Anne when the Princess Royal visited Menagesha in 2003

Both stereotypes contain some truth, of course, but there are exceptions. In the case of CSE, service delivery is a matter of record. During the three years from May 2008-April 2011, CSE operated on a total programme budget (agreed with government departments) of just under Birr 41 million, or £1.52 million - roughly £500,000 a year.

In this three-year period CSE ran the operational centres of Menagesha, Hawassa, Dire Dawa and Harar, undertook the rehabilitation over 300 children at Menagesha, produced nearly 19,000 prosthetic/orthotic devices in its own workshops, and conducted a mobile outreach programme as far as the borders of Kenya, Southern Sudan and Somalia enabling thousands of patients with disabilities to have a regular six-month check and refit. To do such work, CSE employs about 130 people, all Ethiopian nationals. Salaries are not high but job satisfaction is great and staff turnover low.

The organisation's longest-serving employee, its executive director Gebremedhin Bekele, has an almost unbroken record of 40 years with Cheshire. Almost, because he was tempted away a few years ago by an American aid group offering to double his salary – yet he came back. Gebremedhin is, of course, the direct link with Leonard Cheshire. He retains the highest regard for the founder, who he met on several occasions. "The Group Captain was a wise and fine person", he says. "He had no trace of arrogance. He treated everyone fairly."

Derege Legesse had polio as a young boy and was brought to Cheshire by his father, a subsistence farmer. After being operated on he spent a year in rehab at Menagesha. He lived in an orphanage during his secondary school days but won a place at Addis Ababa University. He majored in law and, in his early thirties, became Public Prosecutor for the town of Nazareth. "CSE has transformed my life, but living and working as a handicapped person is a daily struggle," he says. He's seen here with Gebremedhin Bekele

Celebrations marking the golden jubilee of Cheshire in Ethiopia come at a watershed. Lilla Heaslip, former chairman and more recently vice-chairman as well as chair of fundraising, has announced her retirement as of December 2012. Gebremedhin, too, is talking about retirement. The pair have worked together as an exceptional driving force over the past 16 years or so, as Cheshire deliberately set about the transition from being an institution of sorts to becoming a nationwide services deliverer (reflected in the name-change in 2001). As an example of the Anglo-Ethiopian partnership which has reinforced Cheshire locally since day one, theirs is unrivalled.

It is also a time of directional change, as the focus on polio switches to other conditions like club feet. Today, millions of people throughout Ethiopia live, mostly unaided, with treatable disabilities. As described on pages 82-85, Menagesha is now home to rehab for noma patients, with other categories on the way. From its bases at Hawassa, Harar and Dire Dawa, CSE works with families of the disabled in education and income-generation projects. The need, and potential, is enormous.

Cheshire has always sought to stay out of politics and on good terms with government authorities - from Imperial days, through the Derg (when it was the only private charity organisation not to be nationalised) to the present era of Prime Minister Meles Zenawi. President Girma Wolde-Giorgis was, as it happens, chairman of Cheshire Asmara when Eritrea was part of Ethiopia. CSE is recognised as a clean and responsible body, a role model for local NGOs.

That doesn't provide it with a waiver when it comes to observing the law. All land in Ethiopia is owned, or part-owned, by the state. It would be legally possible for Menagesha – originally bequeathed by Princess Tenagnework – to be requisitioned by the government. That won't happen. But when you own nothing, and have budget demands which are continually stretched, it's hard not to get nervous.

CSE welcomes recent NGO law changes which could allow it to generate some income locally. Its approach to the tricky issue of human rights is essentially practical. By helping the disabled in professional ways and contributing to their all-round welfare it underscores the point that they have both rights and responsibilities. It does not campaign.

Advocacy is a different matter. One of CSE's board members, Assefa Ashengo, is a former civil servant who headed the welfare services directorate in the Ministry of Labour and managed a World Bank project reintegrating Eritrean war veterans, some 17,000 of whom were disabled. He argues that perceptions of disability are still very low on the public agenda and believes it is correct to ask federal, regional and local government bodies to set aside more resources, while at the same time challenging negative attitudes to disability in daily life.

Cheshire's board has a reputation for tough-headed realism. After all, the organisation has survived 50 years against the odds. It has seen the end of empire, lived through one of the world's worst periods of genocide, and has adapted to the juggling act expected of NGOs in an aid-dominated environment.

It has established a national rehabilitation service unparalleled by a local NGO in Sub-Saharan Africa. It has developed skills and professional expertise without much recourse to outside agencies or massive grant aid. It has given not just new limbs but new life to thousands of Ethiopians. It looks forward to the next 50 years with confidence.

Gebremedhin sums up his career in this way: "I'm proud of my achievement at Cheshire, though it has been a group effort. We are one of the best organisations in Ethiopia. We are strong, committed and transparent. We have been good for the Leonard Cheshire name." The Group Captain would agree.

Name Index

Abraha, Tesfay 65-66
Able, Nick 24
Alegnta, Zenebech 100
Andom, General Aman Michael 32,34
Andom, Tsion 9,32-33
Anne, Princess Royal 4, 100
Ayele, Fasil 63, 64
Araya, Nahu-Senaye 14,48,86-87
Asheneo, Asefa 102
Assefa, Kifle 65-66
Assefa, Mengistu 65-66
Barron, Tanya 12
Battell, Fr Colin 13,36,44,46-47,48
Bekele, Gebremedhin 4,10,13,20,34,35,38,43,46, 72-74,79,81,84,85,100,101,102
Belete, Hagere 91
Beyissa, Daniel 49-52,84
Bitew, Addis 65-66
Bromley, Lady 27
Buerk, Michael 42
Cheshire, Group Captain Leonard 4,6,8,9,10,12,14,16,19,20,21,22, 23,40, 41,42,43,44,46,72,74,80, 98, 100,102
Damtew, Ras Desta 15
Day, Sir Derek 35, 75
Dekker, Dr Nellie 20
Desta, Commander (Commodore) Iskinder 6,8,9,11,14,15,16,18,34,35
Desta, Princess Ruth 7,15,18,19
Desta, Princess Seble 6,7,8,9,11,14, 15,16,18,19,26,32,34
Desta, Princess Sophie 6,7,8,11,15,18,19,26
Dimbleby, Jonathan 40
Doheny, Fr Kevin 10,40,43,46
Eshete, Prof Enderias 92,94
Eshete, Mamo 10,36,38-39
Evanovitch, Dr Mira 20
Geldof, Bob 12
Gebre, Getachew 42,43
Gebread, Dr Abiye Hailu 85
Geresu, Kebede 58-59
Girma, Desta 10
Glen, Flt Lt 22
Haile, Captain Alemeyu 12,35,36
Haile Selassie, Emperor 6,7,8,9,15,18,20,21,22,26,35
Haile-Selassie, Prince Makonnen 18
Haile-Selassie, Princess Tenagnework 6,7,8,9,11,14,15,18,19,20,22,23,24, 26,38,44,102
Hall, Gillian 7,21,24,35-36,37
Hamlin, Dr Kathryn 82
Hamlin, Dr Reginald 82
Hanna, Abba 19,26
Heaslip, James 80,81
Heaslip, Lilla 4,13,48,75-77,79, 80-81,101
Hitler, Adolf 8
Kelly, Sir Gerald 33
Kennedy, President John F. 35
Kidane, Meseret 68,70
Kifle, Berhanu 96-97
Kifle, Isaac 7,11,35,36,41
Kiflegi, Makeda Aster 9
Kidane, Meseret 68,70
Lawrence, Chris 13, 82-85
Lawrence, Terry 82
Legesse, Derege 101
Lemma, Yehnualeshet 13,48
Lunden, Lorraine 35,36
Lygon, Lady Mary 15
Mabe, Neil 36,38
Mason, Margot 9,19,22
Mariam, Mengistu Haile 9,11,12,32,36,45
Mengesha, Tsige 11
Mengste, Nurlign 62
Moges, Elleni 88-89
Molla, Aychesh 92-95
Muema, Jayne Shanyisa 48
Mussolini, Benito 8
Nibretu, Sisay 90-92
Petch, Sq Ldr Reg 22
Reed, Sir Alec 4,12,13,48,78-79
Robel, Daniel 9,41
Romanovskiy, Dr Evgeny 54
Ryder, Lady Sue 10,12,40,41,42,43,46
Sandford, Christine 18
Sandford, Brigadier Dan 16
Sandford, Pippa 16,43
Selassie, Negussie Wolde 42,44,45,46,48
Shimelis, Tessera Work 43
Steer, George 16
Tabernacle, Denise 6,8,9,16,19,20, 21,26,38,41,43,44,87
Tafessa, Mekuria 12,46
Tassew, Habtamu 58,59
Theresa, Mother 37
Travers, Ronald 12,37,41,43,44,46
Walton, Neil 24-25
Waugh, Alec 15
Waugh, Evelyn 15
Whalley, Joan 30
Wickstead, Myles A 4-5
Wingate, Major-General Orde 16
Wolde-Mariam, Lij Kassa 34
Wolde-Giorgis, President Girma 101
Wood, P.D. 24
Zenawi, Prime Minster Meles 45,46,101

Picture credits (by page)

Cheshire Services Ethiopia: 7,10,79, 88,90,92,96,100
Facing Africa: 83
Leonard Cheshire Disability 17,21, 27,43
Chris Love: 37
UK Crown copyright: 7,10,22,
Robert Waterhouse: 33,39,47,51,53, 55,57,59,61,63,66,67,69,71,73, 77,81,87,101

Menagesha children's drawings
from the Cheshire archive in Derbyshire, UK